REFLECTION: TURNING EXPERIENCE INTO LEARNING

REFLECTION: TURNING EXPERIENCE INTO LEARNING

Edited by David Boud, Rosemary Keogh
and David Walker

 RoutledgeFalmer

Taylor & Francis Group

LONDON AND NEW YORK

First published 1985 and reprinted 1987 by Routledge
2 Park Square, Milton Park, Abingdon, Oxon, OX14 4RN

Reprinted 1994

Transferred to Digital Printing 2005

Routledge Falmer is an imprint of the Taylor & Francis Group

British Library Cataloguing in Publication Data
    Reflection: turning experience into learning.
    1. Learning, Psychology of
    I. Boud, David   II. Keogh, Rosemary
    III. Walker, David
    370.15'23   LB1051
    ISBN 0-85038-864-3

Published in the USA by Nichols Publishing Company,
PO Box 96, New York, NY 10024

Library of Congress Cataloging in Publication Data
    Boud, David.
    Reflection, turning experience into learning.
    Bibliography: p.
    1. Learning — Addresses, essays, lectures. 2. Thought
    and thinking — Addresses, essays, lectures. 3. Students,
    Self-rating of — Addresses, essays, lectures.
    4. Experiential learning — Addresses, essays, lectures.
    I. Title
    LB1060.B68 1985   370.15'23   84-16507
    ISBN 0-85038-864-3

Contents

INTRODUCTION
What is Reflection in Learning?

David Boud, Rosemary Keogh and David Walker

How do you introduce a diverse collection of articles on 'Reflection: Turning Experience into Learning' when many of the contributors have not until now used the term 'reflection' or 'reflection in learning' to describe their own activities? This was the problem which faced us when we met to decide how best to approach our task. We drafted an introduction which gave a straightforward account of what we regarded as reflection, and as we reread it we became increasingly dissatisfied with what we had written. It did not portray any of our intellectual excitement about the issues and it failed to indicate that reflection, as we understand it, is an active process of exploration and discovery which often leads to very unexpected outcomes. As we searched for a new form of expression we began to exchange experiences about what had led us to become so committed to our present project.

All three of us are involved in continuing professional education in various ways and had come to our present positions from very different backgrounds. One of us works in a university and conducts training programmes for university teachers, another works in technical education as a curriculum advisor, and the third is a priest who is responsible for an adult education centre focusing on spiritual development. We had met through membership of an association of teachers and trainers who were involved with experience-based learning. Part of our shared concern was a dissatisfaction with both traditional methods and more recent innovations in teaching together with a desire to promote an awareness in learners of the possibilities for learning and of the need for them to take control of their own learning.

We were convinced that it is important to draw upon learners' prior experience and to provide opportunities for them to be engaged actively in what they are learning. We also agreed, however, that experience alone is not the key to learning. Too often we have seen students subjected to half digested (and half baked) practical work or work experience and to inappropriate academically oriented learning under the guise of professional education and training. What is it that turns experience into learning? What specifically enables learners to gain the maximum benefit from the situations they find themselves in? How can they apply their experiences in new contexts? Why can some learners appear to benefit more than others?

The more we thought about these issues, the more we identified the importance of what we termed 'reflection'. What do we usually imagine when we think of reflection? In the physical sense we think about mirrors and reflected images, of looking and seeing a parallel version of the world. From a human view we may imagine thinking quietly, mulling over events in our mind or making sense of experiences we have had. Groups of people may also come to mind: engaged in reflection either as meditation or prayer or actively discussing recent events and issues. Comparing notes, roundtable discussions, carrying out a post mortem (metaphorically speaking), having an informal group discussion are all used to describe activities with which we are familiar and which have some relation t 'reflection'.

It seems that we all recognize the importance of these activities in our lives. We say that we need time to catch up with ourselves, to take stock, to make sense of what has happened, or to share other peoples' ideas on an experience. These are so commonplace that we regard them as almost natural events in our culture — as natural as breathing. We know intuitively that we need to do these things in order to learn from our experiences and to deal with our expectations.

The activity of reflection is so familiar that, as teachers or trainers, we often overlook it in formal learning settings, and make assumptions about the fact that not only is it occurring, but it is occurring effectively for everyone in the group. It is easy to neglect as it is something which we cannot directly observe and which is unique to each learner, but, as Duley (1981, p611) points out: 'The skill of experiential learning in which people tend to be the most deficient is reflection.' Perhaps if we can sharpen our consciousness of what reflection in learning can involve and how it can be influenced then we may be able to improve our own practice of learning and help those who learn with us.

One approach to improving our understanding of reflection was to examine some of the issues experientially. The Australian Consortium on Experiential Education organizes regular workshops on all aspects of experience-based learning and, in 1982, it devoted its annual one-day conference to the theme 'Reflection: A Neglected Area in Learning'. One of our colleagues planned and conducted the day's activities and led us to begin to consider the issues which were involved. It was a stimulating experience, but one which left us with considerably more questions than we had initially. We became convinced that reflection is a vital element in any form of learning and that teachers and trainers need to consider how they can incorporate some forms of reflection in their courses. Reflection is not a single faceted concept as our conference title had seemed to imply, but a generic term which acts as a shorthand description for a number of important ideas and activities.

Some examples of common learning situations were useful to us in clarifying the idea of reflection in learning. We want to present these and consider them in the light of some simple models of experience-based learning which have been proposed in recent years. Let us examine what might occur in a week-long field trip for geology students, and the clinical placement of a student of child care.

In each case three stages are apparent: preparation, engagement in an activity, and the processing of what has been experienced. In the case of a geology student learning how to conduct a search for oil-bearing strata, the student knows that the aim of the trip is to practise reading the clues on the ground which indicate priorities for further testing of underground content and to become aware of the constraints of field work conditions. Before departing on the trip the teacher will already have briefed the class about the location of the ground search and the exercises which will have to be completed. Lists of equipment, costs to the students, transport and camping arrangements will have been discussed.

In the case of the child care student, placement in a pre-school group might be part of the requirement for the completion of a Child Care Certificate, the aim of the placement being for students to learn about the role of the child care worker in a practical setting. Some of the students will have given some prior thought to the coming experience and will have been encouraged to plan for it by deciding on what they should observe, what questions they should ask, and what skills they should practise. They may talk over these ideas with other students and with their teachers. Many students will be preoccupied with some of the practicalities: what to say to the supervisor of the pre-school on their first meeting, how to handle the unruly child, what clothes to wear and how they should protect themselves from messy fingers.

In both examples the preparatory stage would normally consist of a number of elements:

☐ an outline by the teacher or supervisor of the aims of the activity and the broad structure of what is to take place
☐ students will have the opportunity to seek clarification and perhaps to make modifications to what has been suggested
☐ they will have practised some of the skills required of them in the setting of the college or university
☐ they will be introduced to the resources that are available to assist them during the period of their practical experience.

Depending on the circumstances, and the degree of planning of the course, other preparatory activities may also have occurred (for example, those described in Jenks and Murphy, 1979).

In the preparatory phase reflective activity occurs when students start to explore what is required of them, what are the demands of the field setting and the resources which they themselves have to bring. Typically there would be a relatively high level of anxiety present which some students might respond to by additional preparation and which others might respond to by engaging in a minimal amount of advance planning.

The second phase is the actual field experience. Initially the experience may tend to overwhelm, new observations may rapidly follow each other with insufficient chance for them to be organized and the learner may resort to coping strategies which involve doing what is most familiar. In the child care student's first days he may be confronted with children talking, moving, asking questions, falling over, splashing paint. The geology student may find she has forgotten an implement she needs, she may recognize several complex rock types and find others she has never encountered before. Students may find that field work is more exhausting than they anticipated as they struggle to write up their notes in the tent in the evening. The relationship between this and what they have been taught in the college may be unclear. There is little or no time to think about it and the world of practice appears at first to be totally divorced from the world of the classroom. In a brief field experience of a week or so the students may never come to terms with the relationships between theory and practice. This may not occur for many students until they return to the context of the educational institution and even then they may require a considerable debriefing to make connections and consolidate what they have learned.

The students in our illustrations will have made various kinds of notes and records of their experience. For some this may have taken the form of systematic laboratory notebooks, for others it might have consisted of jottings of events, remarks, questions and thoughts. The input of information may be considerable and students have to draw back from being totally immersed in the experience in order to digest what is happening. This might involve withdrawing for a time from the task, it might involve talking to their colleagues, or trying to make sense of the experience through keeping a personal diary to record issues, feelings and value conflicts.

The third phase comes after the field experience is finished. Students normally have to report on their experience. In the case of a geologist there would often be a fairly well-defined procedure for writing up field notes, but for the child care student the task might not be so clear. In both cases the students will have to refer to their notes and records, to dredge their memories and to try to reconstruct an account of the salient features that they believe are required by their teachers. Even if there are no formal requirements they may wish to do this for themselves so that they can begin to make sense of the experience. In this process the students will realize many things left undone, questions unasked and records incomplete. All this is part of the learning process.

Looking back on these phases we can see many important features. Learners are having to cope with a considerable amount of new information, they are facing personal demands and the situation forces them into active involvement whether they like it or not. Reflection is needed at various points: at the start in anticipation of the experience, during the experience as a way of dealing with the vast array of inputs and coping with the feelings that are generated, and following the experience during the phase of writing and consolidation. Dewey (1933) refers to these as conscious reflective activity. The activity is purposeful although the particular goals may not be clear to the learner or to the teacher at the time. The general goal of reconstructing experience is central, continuing and pervasive. In order to pursue this goal, however, learners need to describe their experience, to work through the attitudes and emotions which might colour their understanding, and to order and make sense of the new ideas and information which they have retained.

We can point to any form of learning activity and demonstrate the reflective phases. Even in formal lecture courses we can see the need for students to process the information they have been given, relate this to their previous knowledge, and test their understanding. However, much of the reflective element in these cases has been formalized and procedures have been established which, although they keep students on the task by giving them tests, assignments and tutorial exercises to do, can tend to relieve them of the responsibility for fully relating to their own framework the inputs which they receive. While this may maximize the amount of cognitive learning as defined by end-of-course examinations, it may inhibit the development of self-organized learning.

If we look back on the illustrations we have given we can identify three points we need to bear in mind. First, and self-evidently, only learners themselves can learn and only they can reflect on their own experiences. Teachers can intervene in various ways to assist, but they only have access to individuals' thoughts and feelings through what individuals choose to reveal about themselves. At this basic level the learner is in total control.

Second, reflection as we have described it is pursued with intent. It is not idle meanderings or day-dreaming, but purposive activity directed towards a goal. This is not to say that it may not be helpful to have periods of reverie and meditation associated with conscious reflection, but in themselves these activities are not what we are referring to when we discuss goal-directed critical reflection.

Third, the reflective process is a complex one in which both feelings and cognition are closely interrelated and interactive. Negative feelings, particularly about oneself, can form major barriers towards learning. They can distort perceptions, lead to false interpretations of events, and can undermine the will to persist. Positive feelings and emotions can greatly enhance the learning process; they can keep the learner on the task and can provide a stimulus for new learning. The affective dimension has to be taken into account when we are engaged in our own learning activities, and when we are assisting others in this process. External influences to validate the worth of individual learners and groups of learners are often needed.

The notion of reflection in learning is not a new one: we found that it can be traced to Aristotle's discussions of practical judgement and moral action in his *Ethics* (Grundy, 1982). In modern times the most influential figure has been that of John Dewey and his use of 'reflective activity' in learning. Dewey (1933) crystallized what many generations of teachers had known and practised intuitively, namely that there were two kinds of experiential process which led to learning. The first process was trial and error which led to 'rule of thumb' decisions. The value to the learner of this kind of process was limited by the specificity of the problem which was solved and the scope of the trial and error explorations. The second process he identified was reflective activity which involved the perception of relationships, and connections between the parts of an experience. Dewey believed that it was this kind of activity that enabled effective problem-solving to take place and that it improved the effectiveness of learning. He explained reflection on experience as if it were a kind of learning loop, continually feeding back and forth between the experience and the relationships being inferred.

In recent years Kolb, Rubin and McIntyre (1971) have added to our thinking through their well-known model of the learning process. The Kolb model is termed an experiential learning model to emphasize the important part that experience plays in the learning process, an emphasis which differentiates this approach from other cognitive theories of the learning process (Kolb, 1976). The core of the model is a simple description of the learning cycle: how experience is translated into concepts, which in turn are used as guides in the choice of new experiences. Learning is conceived of as a four stage cycle. Immediate concrete experience is the basis for observation and reflection, these observations are assimilated into a theory from which new implications for action can be deduced and these implications or hypotheses are used to indicate new experiences (see Figure 1).

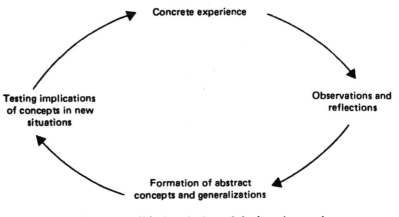

Figure 1 *Kolb's description of the learning cycle*
(Kolb and Fry, 1975)

Kolb argues that learners, if they are to be effective, need four different kinds of abilities which correspond to the four stages of his learning cycle: concrete experience abilities, reflective observation abilities, abstract conceptualization abilities and active experimentation abilities. These abilities represent the contrasting elements of the two major dimensions of cognitive growth and learning: the concrete/abstract dimension and the active/reflective dimension. Any individual will have strengths in particular parts of these dimensions and will need to develop the skills to operate along the full range if they are to be effective. Kolb has developed a learning style inventory to enable learners to discover their own characteristics in these dimensions (Kolb and Fry, 1975).

Unfortunately Kolb does not discuss the nature of his stage of observation and reflection in much detail. It can appear to refer to the act of associating an incoming idea with one already in the mind of the observer. His scheme has been useful in assisting us in planning learning activities and in helping us check simply that learners can be effectively engaged by the tasks we have set. It does not help, however, to uncover the elements of reflection itself.

Another simple model which gives reflection a central place is that proposed by the British Further Education Curriculum and Development Unit (FEU) in their guide, *Experience, Reflection, Learning*. The FEU model has three phases: the experience of the learner, the specific learning which occurs on the basis of that experience, and the reflective activities which are needed to extract specific learning from the overall experience (see Figure 2).

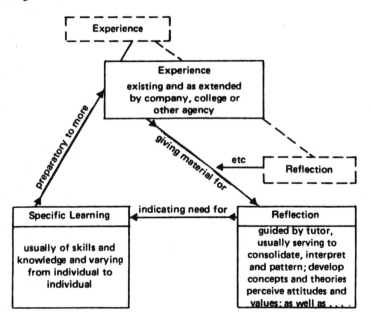

Figure 2 *FEU model*

The FEU authors' view of the role of reflection in their model is:

> The individual's experience needs to be followed by some organised reflection. This reflection enables the individual to learn from the experience, but also helps identify any need for some specific learning before further experience is acquired. (FEU, 1981, p21)

Like Kolb they do not explore the nature of the reflective activity other than to indicate that it includes crystallizing and reinforcing previous learning, developing concepts and generalizations for future use, processes of interpretation and perception of values. Their stress on organized reflection points to the purposive or intentioned nature of the reflective activity, that it is not aimless. They also emphasize a 'whole person' view of the learner and include in their notion of reflection the processing of feelings, values and attitudes as well as the cognitive and psycho-motor aspects of the experience.

Grundy (1982) provides us with a third view of the place of reflection in learning. She considers the experience of a person within the context of a group of autonomous learners with a common learning objective or purpose. As in the Kolb and FEU models, in Grundy's approach the learners have a clear purpose in reflecting on an experience, which may be a shared event or episode.

She has pointed to several places in the learning process where reflective activity occurs. Each person, interacting with other group members, brings their informed practical judgement to bear on ideas relevant to the event. This episode of researching and evaluating ideas is reflection in her view and results in new knowledge and ideas. A further phase of reflection may occur to re-examine more basic assumptions, and deeper insights might develop. These new insights may then be applied to the original event or to other relevant events in more reflective activity. These phases of reflection may be sequential, may overlap, be simultaneous, and some may be omitted.

Grundy also attempts to describe the nature of reflection. In this she adopts a functional approach as does the FEU. What is interesting and different in her work is that she focuses on the relationships which must be obtained between teacher and students and among students if critical reflection is to occur. One of the key features of self-reflection is the need for people to have the freedom to make a genuine choice for themselves, rather than conform to the influence of the teacher or other students. For this to happen, she argues that there must be a structure which allows equal power relationships between group members, including the teacher or facilitator, if the freedom to choose is to be a valid one.

Once we had developed a context and some examples of reflection in learning a plan began to emerge for a publication which would bring together the disparate and diverse writings on the topic of reflection in learning and provide a focus for further exploration. At first this was conceived as a series of papers which would circulate among those particularly interested in the subject. As we talked further to our friends and colleagues, however, it became apparent that the need we had felt was experienced more widely than we had anticipated, and we were encouraged to turn our modest ideas into a book.

Our plan was to identify those people who, in our view, had made an important contribution to thinking and practice in the area of reflection in learning, ask them to write an account of the approaches to reflection with which they were most familiar and discuss the issues which they considered to be important.

This ultimately led to the present book. Our aim is to focus attention on reflection in learning by bringing together diverse trends in educational ideas and practices with a view to encouraging teachers and learners to adopt a clear view on the role of reflection in their own teaching and learning and consider the range of approaches which is available to them. Specifically we aim to acquaint people with information about different types of reflective activity and areas relating to the process of reflection, by describing what educators are doing and what they consider to be crucial issues.

We want to reach those who wish to develop their own educational practices further by drawing upon the experience of participants in their programmes, both their prior experience and that provided by the programme or course itself. These areas would include project work, on-the-job training, practical work, field study, internships, clinical training, pastoral work, educational gaming and simulation and other forms of experiential learning. We believe that this book will be useful to those who wish to collaborate with others in learning, whether they be students or peers. It will also be of particular interest to those who wish to direct their own learning in conjunction with others, through co-operative inquiry, action research projects, and learning communities.

The contributors have been chosen from very diverse areas. These include management education, teacher training, professional development, spiritual development, medical education, technical training, psychology, adult and continuing education and study counselling. In their own fields they have all been involved in developing activities which have been brought together here under the heading of reflection in learning. They have direct personal experience of the processes they discuss and they can link them to a broader framework.

We have asked them to keep in mind the basic question: what has my work to contribute to an understanding of reflection in learning and how might reflection be facilitated? The core of each chapter is an account of specific ideas, methods and approaches to reflection in specific contexts. They have also been asked to provide a clear rationale for their approach and to indicate any underlying theory and concepts in a way which does not require any specialist background from the reader.

The book has been structured to provide, in the first chapter, a general overview of some of the main ideas. This is followed by accounts of particular approaches and applications. Applications are of two types: the first to conventional teaching or training situations in which the teacher essentially directs or guides the learning process, and the second, to co-operative inquiry in which groups of people work together on a particular project without necessarily identifying themselves as consciously involved in learning.

In the first chapter 'Promoting Reflection in Learning: a Model', we explore what is meant by reflection in learning and how the idea of reflection in learning relates to other important ideas in the planning of learning activities. This chapter provides a framework within which the various aspects of reflection can be considered. We discuss the essential relationship between learning experiences and reflection on them. The elements of reflection are teased out and presented in terms of a model.

John Powell in Chapter 2, 'Autobiographical Learning', examines the use of autobiographical techniques in assisting learners to come to an awareness of learning and explores the concept of learning through autobiography. He describes how learners can create and use their own autobiographies to come to deeper appreciations of the process of learning. Autobiographies are one form of reflection through writing. David Walker in Chapter 3, 'Writing and Reflection', looks at other methods such as the keeping of diaries, journals and portfolios. He describes how portfolios can be used in educational settings and discusses issues which arise for the teacher or trainer who wishes to employ them.

Reflection does not have to be a solitary activity. It can occur in group settings as well as through individual writing and thinking. The most familiar area in which reflection occurs in groups is when debriefing takes place. Debriefing occurs when participants in a learning activity, be it a simulation, workshop experience or other event, are led through a session in which they relive parts of their experience in a supportive environment and draw conclusions from it. A great deal of work on educational gaming and simulation has stressed the importance of debriefing, but it is a practice which is often given much less attention than its proponents claim it should warrant. Margot Pearson and David Smith in Chapter 4, 'Debriefing in Experience-based Learning', focus on this issue and try to identify why it is that debriefings are not always well conducted, and propose ways in which they can be made more effective.

Between individual activity and working in a group is one-to-one learning. How can one individual help another to reflect on their learning? Susan Knights in Chapter 5, 'Reflection and Learning: the Importance of a Listener', highlights the role of attentive listening and the need for the support of others in learning and reflection.

While most of the contributors focus on a particular approach and illustrate this with reference to their practice, Alex Main in Chapter 6, 'Reflection and the Development of Learning Skills', examines the area of assisting students develop effective learning skills, that is, how students can be helped to learn how to learn. The most productive ways in his experience have been those in which students reflect critically on their own practices rather than through prescriptions of 'good' learning practice.

The idea of a learning conversation is described by Philip Candy, Sheila Harri-Augstein and Laurie Thomas in Chapter 7, 'Reflection and the Self-organized Learner'. This is a specific approach to enable learners to examine their own learning in a systematic manner and uncover their own assumptions and constructs about what they are doing. They are influenced by the work of George Kelly on personal construct psychology and they use one of the techniques which has arisen from his work, the repertory grid, as the means for learners to identify and question their own strategies.

Not all learning occurs in formal settings. Indeed, most takes place as a part of everyday life, either as part of work or of other activities. Philip Boxer is involved with management education, and he is concerned about the development of skills of judgement and decision-making. In Chapter 8, 'Judging the Quality of Development', he proposes a teaching paradigm to suggest how managers can reflect outside the boundaries of their normal perspectives.

In Chapter 9 by John Heron, 'The Role of Reflection in Co-operative Inquiry', the focus is on learning through collaboration with others. In this a group of people attempt collectively to explore an issue which is important to them both through familiar research techniques and through reflective analysis of their progress. Heron shows how this can be effectively conducted in the context of an experiential learning cycle.

Chapter 10, 'Action Research and the Politics of Reflection' by Stephen Kemmis, acts as an endpiece. He takes the view that critical reflection is a social and political activity as well as a psychological one and maintains that reflection is not purely an internal process; it is action-oriented and embedded in a cultural and historical context. For him reflection is a political act which is shaped by ideology as, in turn, ideology shapes reflection. Any reflective activities which fail to take these factors into account are limited and may be misguided. He ends with a plea for research on reflection which engages individuals and groups in collaborative action research.

We are convinced that the concept of reflection is an important and practical one in education. Although it is interpreted in various ways it does point to an important dimension which has been undervalued. We hope that this book will provide a starting point for those who wish to explore this area further.

References

Dewey, J (1933) *How We Think*, Boston: D C Heath

Duley, J S (1981) Field experience education, in Chickering, A W (ed) *The Modern American College*, San Francisco: Jossey-Bass

Further Education Curriculum and Development Unit (1981) *Experience, Reflection, Learning*, London: Department of Education and Science, Further Education Unit

Grundy, S (1982) Three modes of action research, *Curriculum Perspectives*, **2**, 3, pp23-34

Jenks, C L and Murphy, C J (1979) *Experience-Based Learning and the Facilitative Role of the Teacher*, San Francisco: Far West Laboratory for Educational Research and Development

Kolb, D A (1976) Management and the learning process, *California Management Review*, **18**, 3, pp21-31

Kolb, D A and Fry, R (1975) Towards an applied theory of experiential learning, in Cooper, C L (ed) *Theories of Group Processes*, London: John Wiley, pp33-58

Kolb, D A, Rubin, I and McIntyre, J (1971) *Organizational Psychology: An Experiential Approach*, Englewood Cliffs, New Jersey: Prentice-Hall

CHAPTER 1

Promoting Reflection in Learning: a Model

David Boud, Rosemary Keogh and David Walker

Introduction

In the Introduction we presented some illustrations of the role of reflection in common learning situations. We are now in a position to present our own model of reflection in learning. We have been led to this by an analysis of examples of the kind discussed above, by our own experience of the processes of learning and the work of a number of authors who have considered reflection as a part of learning.

We wish to restrict our scope to what Tough (1979) terms 'deliberate' learning. That is, learning which is intentional in which learners are aware that they are learning; learning with a definite, specific goal rather than generalized learning, for example, to 'develop the mind'; learning which is undertaken in order to pursue this goal; and learning which the individual intends to retain (Knapper and Cropley, in press). Of course much of our discussion may also apply to other less conscious or less organized forms of learning, but these involve other considerations which would take us away from our main area of interest. Deliberate learning occurs within educational and training institutions, but a great deal takes place on a less formal basis away from these institutions (Tough, 1979). In addition we wish to focus primarily on experiential or experience-based learning (Boud and Pascoe, 1978) rather than what Coleman (1976) refers to as classroom learning which concerns symbolic or information assimilation, although we believe that similar considerations might also apply in these latter areas.

Reflection is a form of response of the learner to experience. In our model we have indicated two main components: the experience and the reflective activity based upon that experience. In the sense in which we are using the term, experience consists of the total response of a person to a situation or event: what he or she thinks, feels, does and concludes at the time and immediately thereafter. The situation or event could be part of a formal course, eg a workshop, a field trip, a lecture; or it could be more informal: an event arising from a personal study project or from the actions of a community group, or a totally unplanned occurrence in daily life. It could be provoked by an external agent or it could be an internal experience, arising out of some discomfort with one's present state. In

18

most cases the initial experience is quite complex and is constituted of a number of particular experiences within it. In the case of the child care student discussed in the Introduction, the learning experience would consist of the time spent within the classroom, but within that there would be many observations, thoughts, perceptions, reactions, awkward moments, and interchanges which would make up the total experience.

After the experience there occurs a processing phase: this is the area of reflection. Reflection is an important human activity in which people recapture their experience, think about it, mull it over and evaluate it. It is this working with experience that is important in learning. The capacity to reflect is developed to different stages in different people and it may be this ability which characterizes those who learn effectively from experience. Why is it that conscious reflection is necessary? Why can it not occur effectively at the unconscious level? It can and does occur, but these unconscious processes do not allow us to make active and aware decisions about our learning. It is only when we bring our ideas to our consciousness that we can evaluate them and begin to make choices about what we will and will not do. For these reasons it is important for the learner to be aware of the role of reflection in learning, and how the processes involved can be facilitated. Some authors (for example, Taylor, 1981) present reflection as a stage in the learning process which occurs after substantial other activity has taken place, towards the latter part of a one-semester course, for instance. While we accept that major periods of reflection may take place in this manner we also wish to include in our definition more modest reflective activities which may occur daily.

In our view, reflection in the context of learning is a generic term for those intellectual and affective activities in which individuals engage to explore their experiences in order to lead to new understandings and appreciations. It may take place in isolation or in association with others. It can be done well or badly, successfully or unsuccessfully. However, we wish to focus on what learners and teachers can do to ensure that it is a productive experience.

Probably, for adult learners, most events which precipitate reflection arise out of the normal occurrences of one's life. The impetus may arise from a loss of confidence in or disillusionment with one's existing situation. This could be provoked by an external event, or could develop from one's own reflection on a whole series of occurrences over time, causing a dissatisfaction which leads to a reconsideration of them. Boyd and Fales (1983) refer to this experience as an 'inner discomfort', and Dewey writes of:

> a state of doubt, hesitation, perplexity, mental difficulty, in which [reflective] thinking originates, and . . . an act of searching, hunting, inquiring, to find material that will resolve the doubt, settle and dispose of the perplexity. (Dewey, 1933, p12)

Reflection may also be prompted by more positive states, for example, by an experience of successfully completing a task which previously was thought impossible. This may stimulate a reappraisal of other tasks and the

19

planning of new experiences. For someone who has acquired some facility in reflection, the personal affective aspect would be a more frequent impetus rather than particular activities planned by others.

We believe that the more teachers and learners understand this reflective aspect of learning and organize learning activities which are consistent with it, the more effective learning can be. The model points to the starting point and objects of reflection: the totality of experiences of learners, the behaviour in which they have engaged, the ideas of which learners are aware and the feelings which they have experienced. It designates the outcomes of reflection, which may be a personal synthesis, integration and appropriation of knowledge, the validation of personal knowledge, a new affective state, or the decision to engage in some further activity. It also points to the various intellectual and affective processes involved in reflection. These may be facilitated by individual learners or, in some cases, by others assisting them in learning. Figure 1 presents this diagrammatically.

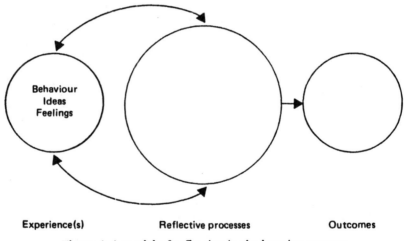

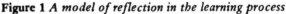

Experience(s)　　　　　Reflective processes　　　　　Outcomes

Figure 1 *A model of reflection in the learning process*

In discussing the model we will for the sake of simplicity refer to the initial learning experience as if it were a singular event; we will also assume in talking about reflection that a particular event has occurred which is the focus of reflection. Of course, in practice we all have a number of experiences over a period of time some of which will become the focus of reflection and some of which will not; often these will not be perceived as separate incidents and it may not be possible for us to identify a particular event which acts as a trigger. However, the general features of reflection in such circumstances are similar. Although we have defined the scope of what we term reflection, and we believe that this corresponds generally to current usage, other authors use different terms for this concept. For example, van Manen (1977) following the German tradition uses the word 'experience', and More (1974) uses 'learning'.

Despite all that has been written about reflection it is difficult to be precise about the nature of the process. It is so integral to every aspect of learning that in some way it touches most of the processes of the mind. As yet little research has been conducted on reflection in learning and that which has been undertaken offers few guidelines for the practical problems which face us as teachers and learners. However, it is possible to extract some principles from those who have examined their own learning processes.

John Dewey wrote a great deal about what he referred to as reflective thought and, in common with a number of philosophers who have discussed reflection (cf Ryle), he assumed it was highly rational and controlled. He defined reflective thought as:

> Active, persistent, and careful consideration of any belief or supposed form of knowledge in the light of the grounds that support it and further conclusions to which it leads . . . it includes a conscious and voluntary effort to establish belief upon a firm basis of evidence and rationality. (Dewey, 1933, p9)

Dewey considered that reflection involves an integration of attitudes and skills in methods of inquiry; that neither attitudes nor skills alone will suffice (Zeichner, 1982). Although we acknowledge a great debt to Dewey, we do not fully follow his path. In particular we give much greater emphasis to the affective aspects of learning, the opportunities these provide for enhancing reflection and the barriers which these pose to it.

In order to explore this model in more detail we shall consider each aspect of it in turn and focus on those issues which in our view are important in ensuring that the process of reflection is an effective one. First, we will examine some of the characteristics of learners and the significance of these for their response to the initial experience. As by definition the experience which will be processed has to be experienced by the individual, what the learner brings to the event is essential to an understanding of what occurs. Second, we will look at what we regard as the three major elements of the reflective process itself: returning to the experience, attending to feelings, and re-evaluating the experience. These elements are concerned with how the learner works on the experience, links new knowledge with old, re-examines the initial experience in the light of his or her own goals, integrates learning into his or her existing framework, and rehearses it with a view to subsequent activity.

The Learner

The characteristics and aspirations of the learner are the most important factors in the learning process. The response of the learner to new experience is determined significantly by past experiences which have contributed to the ways in which the learner perceives the world. The way one person reacts to a given situation will not be the same as others and this becomes more obvious when learners from diverse backgrounds work together.

Those who approach the new learning experience from a history of success in similar situations may be able to enter more fully into the new context and draw more from it. The person who is adequately prepared in the particular area of learning can approach it with feelings of competence and confidence and is more likely to find it a rewarding experience at the time and will be drawn into it more easily. A history of positive associations with teachers can also contribute to productive involvements in new learning experiences. The building of a good climate in which to conduct learning activities is directed towards bringing these positive attitudes to the fore.

It is also necessary to take into account negative experiences from the past. An example of the unique response of an individual and how this can affect teaching plans is shown by a recent incident. In one of our classes a group of adults was shown a film about the life of the German theologian, Dietrich Bonhoeffer. It was intended that this should stimulate discussion on some of the values implicit in his work. After the film there was a period of discussion in small groups focusing on a series of questions provided to help each participant formulate his or her own response to the values presented. After the exercise was complete the group commented on the activity. Most of them had responded to the film in the way anticipated by the teacher. However, in one case the entire experience had been quite different. During the film there had been very brief flashes of atrocities inflicted in concentration camps: these appeared to have been included to provide a background for the issues presented in the film. However, they were sufficient to arouse in one participant a reaction quite unlike that of the others. This person, as a child, had experienced at first hand atrocities similar to those portrayed, and the film's brief flashes of them had caused her to relive those past events. Her response to the intellectual values presented in the film had been drowned in the emotional upsurge that had been triggered in her. The teacher's facilitation of reflection on the experience of the film in no way related to what this person had experienced, and, for her, the whole exercise was of a dramatically different nature from that of the others.

This example may appear a little atypical, but in all situations we find that our perceptions of events are conditioned by past experience which has shaped our response to the world around us, and that knowledge of how this has affected us in unknown or unknowable to a teacher. Less vivid examples of the above occur every day in other ways. A student who has had unpleasant experiences in, say, a mathematics or science class may, when exposed to similar situations in the future, experience again the same feelings of discomfort. These can interfere with the process of subject-matter learning as the student may become so preoccupied with emotional reactions that the new information presented by the teacher is not clearly perceived. The learner does not relate to the mathematical or scientific content but rather responds covertly to the past humiliation and embarrassment. This emotional load can carry over into the learner's processing of the subject, and unless some way can be found of resolving these feelings there will be no new learning of the content in question. Such negative reactions to formal classroom situations are more common than we usually care to admit. Of course, there are also the mathematics students who have had enjoyable experiences and for whom maths is fun. After the particular class is over they continue holding their positive attitude; they may be good at mathematics not because of any special natural ability but because they feel comfortable about learning it.

George Kelly (1955) in his personal construct theory refers to the individual and unique perception of each person. He highlights the differences in individual perception and response to the one event and identifies the need for teachers to be aware that what is in their heads is not necessarily translated to the heads of their students. In Kelly's view objects, events or concepts are only meaningful when seen from the perspective of the person construing their meaning. This suggests that techniques to assist reflection need to be applied to the constructions of the learner, rather than those of the teacher. A similar emphasis can be found in the work of Paulo Freire (1970) although he stressed cultural rather than psychological factors in learning. His team of literacy workers adopted the view that learners have a personal perception of the world which is culturally induced, so that their personal meanings or constructs can only be comprehended in their unique social and political context. Both Kelly and Freire highlight the centrality of individuals' perceptions in learning. As Abbs (1974) puts it, 'one must again and again return to the person before us'.

One of the most important areas of learning for adults is that which frees them from their habitual ways of thinking and acting and involves them in what Mezirow (1978, 1981) terms 'perspective transformation'. This means the process of becoming critically aware of how and why our assumptions about the world in which we operate have come to constrain the way we see ourselves and our relationships. He suggests that there are two paths to perspective transformation: one is a sudden insight into the structure of the assumptions which have limited or distorted one's understanding of oneself and one's relationships; the other is directed towards the same end but it proceeds more slowly by a series of transitions which permit one to revise specific assumptions about oneself and others until a stage occurs in which the assumptions become transformed. Freire (1970) has used the term 'conscientization' to describe the process by which one's false consciousness becomes transcended through education. In a similar context Reed (1981, cited in Cunningham, 1983) discusses what he calls 'the empowering learning process' which assumes that problems for individual learners may have their source in the structures of society. In Reed's view 'the essence of such an empowering process is the transformation of social consciousness' and this involves focusing on the social experience of learners and the historical development of society. Lessons are drawn from these in order to improve learners' own practice.

The Learner's Intent

The intentions of the learner are particularly important; often a desire to learn for a particular purpose can assist in overcoming many obstacles and inhibitions. Intentions also influence a learner's approach to a situation and the ways which are chosen to process experience. When the activity being processed is one which is shared with others the intentions of the group may be paramount and it will then be necessary to take into account the potentially divergent goals within the group.

The learner can choose to direct reflective activity to a variety of ends. These intentions can influence both the manner of reflection and its outcome. They can be directed towards exploring organized knowledge, towards self-exploration, or examining the natural and human environment or context in which the learner is operating. For example, in the case of the geology field trip discussed in the| Introduction, the processing of the experience might be directed towards the study of geological strata, to the practicalities of working under field conditions, to the learner's response to these conditions or, indeed, to all of these. The outcomes of these might be an improved conceptualization of particular rock features, a greater awareness of the use of certain surveying techniques, the development of a lack of confidence in coping with the field environment, or a reappraisal of the desire to become a field-based geologist. The intent of the learner permeates every stage of the process from the choice to engage in a particular activity to the ultimate results of the reflective process. Recollection of the event itself will be affected by it because, in the replaying of the experience, particular attention may be given to those elements which appear to be relevant to the goals of the learner.

Intentions vary both between individuals and within an individual depending on the task at hand. Researchers who have studied university students have identified approaches to learning which they have classified as either deep or surface approaches. The deep approach is one in which students seek an understanding of the meaning of what they are studying, relate it to their previous knowledge and interact actively with the material at hand. In contrast, those who adopt a surface approach tend to memorize information and focus on the requirements of tests and examinations (Säljö, 1981; Gibbs et al 1982). Entwistle and Ramsden describe the deep approach as being characterized by an integration of formal learning with personal experience, the formation of relationships between parts of knowledge, and a search for meaning, and the surface approach as the treatment of tasks as unrelated, an emphasis on memorization and an attitude of unreflectiveness (Entwistle and Ramsden, 1983). However, these approaches are not constant in any one student and someone might adopt a deep or a surface approach depending on the circumstances and their intentions at the time (Entwistle and Ramsden, 1983). The adoption of a reflective approach is a choice which we can make or not as we wish, and is one which can be associated with the deep approach to learning.

The importance of intent has been recognized in modern work on reflection. For Dewey (1916) reflection is a process which perceives connections and links between the parts of an experience. He thought that the context of reflection is uncertainty in the environment and that the learner's activity in that context is 'an intentional effort . . . to discover specific connections' which will improve certainty. For Jurgen Habermas (1974) an important reflective process occurs in a context of purpose which he calls 'critical intent'. He sees this as the disposition to investigate and reconstruct an aspect of the social and moral environment to achieve enlightenment and ultimately emancipation. In his view a group of persons with critical intent bringing their informed judgement to bear on the apparent issues or problem is an act of reflection. This process generates critical ideas or theories about the validity of the questions which are considered and the inferences which are drawn, and the reconstruction of new ones. Reflective activity with critical intent is, for Habermas, the heart of the process which frees the human mind.

Mezirow (1981) has used the framework of Habermas in his studies of adult learning and has given the concept of critical reflectivity a central role. Critical reflectivity plays a vital part in this demanding activity and Mezirow (1981) describes some of the major dimensions of this concept in his important theoretical paper.

At the first level there are the forms of reflectivity of our ordinary consciousness which Mezirow defines in the following way. *Reflectivity* is the act of becoming aware of a specific perception, meaning or behaviour of our own or of habits we have of seeing, thinking or acting; *affective reflectivity* is becoming aware of how we feel about the way we are perceiving, thinking or acting or about our habits of doing so. *Discriminant reflectivity* is assessing the efficacy of our perceptions, thoughts, actions and habits of doing things: identifying immediate causes; recognizing reality contexts (a play, game, dream, or religious, musical or drug experience, etc) in which we are functioning and identifying our relationships in the situation. There is also *judgemental reflectivity*, which is making and becoming aware of our value judgements about our perceptions, thoughts, actions and habits in terms of their being liked or disliked, beautiful or ugly, positive or negative.

There are also forms of reflectivity which pertain particularly to perspective transformation and to our critical consciousness. *Conceptual reflectivity* is becoming conscious of our awareness and critiquing it as, for example, when we question the constructs we are using when we evaluate another person. *Psychic reflectivity* is recognizing in oneself the habit of making precipitant judgements about people on the basis of limited information about them, and recognizing the interests and anticipations which influence the way we perceive, think or act.

These latter two aspects of critical consciousness may be differentiated from *theoretical reflectivity* which Mezirow believes is central to perspective transformation. *Theoretical reflectivity* is becoming aware that the reason for a habit of precipitant judgement or for conceptual inadequacy is a set of taken-for-granted cultural or psychological

assumptions which explain personal experience less satisfactorily than
another perspective with more functional criteria for seeing, thinking
and acting.

Promoting Reflection

We want now to look at the process of reflection from the point of view of
the learner and put special emphasis on the relationship of the reflective
process to the learning experience and on what learners can do, with and
without the aid of others, to enhance this activity.

   In our view, one of the most important ways to enhance learning is to
strengthen the link between the learning experience and the reflective
activity which follows it. At the simplest level this link can be formed by
incorporating into learning activities a specific allocation of time which
can be used for reflection. This can be achieved, for example, by the
scheduling of a debriefing period for a group or by setting specific time
aside for keeping a diary of events and one's reactions to them. If we are
exposed to one new event after another without a break we are unlikely
to be able to make the most of any of the events separately. The link can
also be formed through the application of various techniques to aid
reflection during the time that has been set aside. We start from the
position that it is useful for learners and teachers to have a model of
reflection which points to some of the major processes which they should
consider, for them to have their attention drawn to the importance of
reflective activity, and for them to plan consciously for the reflective
stage of the learning process.

   Figure 2 lists the three elements which we believe are important in the
reflective process. *Returning to experience* is simply the recollection of
the salient events, the replaying of the initial experience in the mind of
the learner or the recounting to others of the features of the experience.
Attending to feelings has two aspects: utilizing positive feelings and
removing obstructing feelings. Utilization of positive feelings involves
focusing on positive feelings about learning and the experience which
is subject to reflection. This may involve the conscious recollection of
good experiences, attention to pleasant aspects of the immediate
environment, or the anticipation of the possible benefits to be derived
from the processing of events. Removing obstructing feelings is a necessary
precursor to a rational consideration of events. This may involve
expressing one's feelings when recounting an event to others by, for
example, laughing through the tale of an embarrassing incident or
through some other form of catharsis. It involves whatever needs to be
done in order to remove impediments to a thorough examination of
the experience.

   This leads to the third stage of *re-evaluating experience* which, although
it is the most important, is often not completed if the preceding two are
omitted. Some form of evaluation might have taken place at the time of
the experience and may in the learner's mind be part of the experience

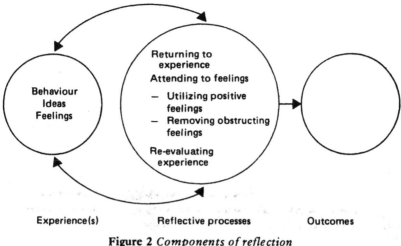

Figure 2 *Components of reflection*

itself. Re-evaluation involves re-examining experience in the light of the learner's intent, associating new knowledge with that which is already possessed, and integrating this new knowledge into the learner's conceptual framework. It leads to an appropriation of this knowledge into the learner's repertoire of behaviour. This can involve a rehearsal in which the new learning is applied mentally to test its authenticity and the planning of subsequent activity in which this learning is applied in one's life. Although we have separated these elements and stages within each it is not possible to regard them as distinct and unrelated. In general, the process may tend to proceed in the sequence we have described, but this may involve many cycles between stages, repetitions of important elements and lingering over particularly significant components.

Stage 1 Returning to Experience
One of the most useful activities that can initiate a period of reflection is recollecting what has taken place and replaying the experience in the mind's eye, to observe the event as it has happened and to notice exactly what occurred and one's reactions to it in all its elements. It may be helpful to commit this description to paper, or to describe it to others. By whatever means this occurs the description should involve a close attention to detail and should refrain from making judgements. As one replays the experience chronologically, details usually begin to emerge which were ignored at the time of the experience, or only noted in passing. As we witness the events again they become available for us to reconsider and examine afresh; we realize what we were feeling and what responses prompted us to act as we did. This description provides the data for subsequent processing and can help to ensure that our reflection is on

27

the basis of the actual events as we experienced them at the time, rather than in terms of what we wished had happened.

For example, the geology student may, at the end of the field trip, start to think about preparing a report and as a preliminary review her experience by recalling each day in the field. To aid her in this she may turn to her field notes to prompt her and help her reconstruct past events: 'why did I write this?', 'what was happening when I observed that?', 'I was really excited when that occurred'. Only part of this recollection will be of immediate use to her in writing her report, but the exercise helps her to focus on the experience and to extract from it what is important. Recollection may need to be repeated many times and from many perspectives; for example, once focusing on the external events, again noticing one's feelings, and again becoming aware of the ideas associated with it.

The simple replay of events and responses logically precedes any cogitation although in any given situation they may be interlinked. What takes place first is a clarification of the personal perceptions of the learner. The learner stands back from the immediacy of the experience and whatever personal challenge it may have been at the time and reviews it with the leisure of not having to act on it in real time. The learner can then start to view the experience from other perspectives, perhaps to see herself as others see her, or to stand back metaphorically to look at the wider context in which the event was situated. The review may not take long if it is done mentally; if it proves fruitful it can be developed to whatever length is desired.

The description of the experience should be, as far as possible, clear of any judgements as these tend to cloud our recollections and may blind us to some of the features which we may need to reassess. However, what can emerge in the descriptive process is the observation of judgements and interpretations which took place at the time of the experience itself or shortly thereafter. Often false perceptions can be detected by recollection alone. One of the main reasons for writing descriptions or reporting them to others is to provide a check on whether they are free from judgements. Debriefing is a technique which can be used for individuals or for groups which begins by a lengthy period of description and returns to the original experience before proceeding to any analysis (see Chapter 4).

Of particular importance within description is the observation of the feelings evoked during the experience. On occasions our emotional reactions can override our rationality to such an extent that we react unawarely and with blurred perceptions or they may foster the development of confidence and a sense of self-worth that can lead us to pursue paths which previously may have been unavailable to us. It is useful to recognize that this is occurring even though it may not be appropriate to focus further on these at this stage. Acknowledging feelings, whether experienced as positive or negative, can enable us to enter into the second and third phases of reflection more easily. Learners who do not observe this affective dimension of their experience may undermine the value of their reflections by restricting them to one aspect of their response to the world around them, thus placing artificial barriers on their response to experience.

At any stage insights might arise 'out of the blue'. They may be instantaneous or intuitive appreciations of an important truth, or enriched descriptions of the events. They cannot be planned, but they may signal the beginning of a new level of reflection which involves working with the insight as well as the recollections of experience and they may also involve re-evaluation and the making of judgements.

Stage 2 Attending to Feelings

It has already been noted that describing events can bring us to an awareness of the feelings that were present during the initial experience. In the example given earlier about the reactions of a viewer of the Bonhoeffer film, the emotional response of the learner to the film drowned the response which had been anticipated by the teacher. Even though our emotions and feelings are a significant source of learning, they can also at times become barriers. Depending on the circumstances and our intentions we need either to work with our emotional responses, find ways of setting them aside, or if they are positive ones retaining and enhancing them. If they do form barriers, these need to be recognized as such and removed before the learning process can proceed.

Utilizing our positive feelings is particularly important as they can provide us with the impetus to persist in what might be very challenging situations, they can help us see events more sharply and they can provide the basis for new affective learning. Unless we believe in ourselves and our own capabilities we can constrain ourselves to such an extent that we deny ourselves learning opportunities and fail to extract what is available to us in any given situation. Our geology student would not be able to go about all the technical tasks effectively if she did not feel that she could cope well with the basic requirements of living in the field. Positive feelings can be enhanced through attending to situations in which we have been successful or in which we have felt good about ourselves. We can focus on what we regarded as good about the experience and appreciate those things we did which were worthwhile, creative or stimulating. If we can establish a positive affective state we are able to pursue both cognitive learning and to develop our emotional lives.

Sometimes in reflection we are not able to recollect events clearly, or we may be so rooted in one perspective or fixed on a given interpretation, that we give up reflection believing that we have reached an understanding of the experience. Commonly what has happened is that an affective barrier has been raised which has temporarily disabled us. Heron (1982) suggests that what is happening is that our 'human capacities' cease to respond flexibly and creatively to the current situation as it is'. When this occurs, the feelings in question need to be discharged or transformed in a way that enables us to regain our flexibility and creativity in responding to the current situation. It is not enough to repress these distorting feelings. While this may remove them from our consciousness, it does not remove the potentially debilitating effects that they have on our mental processes.

These issues need to be handled sensitively. They need to be resolved in a way that will remove their undesirable influence and will facilitate continued support for future learning. They can be discharged by being expressed openly in a sustaining environment, for example on a one-to-one basis or within some kind of support group, so that an emotional obstacle can be removed through, for example, laughing, animated speech, anger or crying (Heron, 1982). Some people can discharge them, in the view of Rainer (1980), through forms of writing. Through such approaches learners can be freed from the mental bonds which were acting as constraints on them and they may be able to respond freely, flexibly and creatively once again. Not all authors, however, would regard discharge as the most appropriate avenue in the situations we can consider. An alternative way is through the transmutation of emotions through various meditative techniques (Heron, 1982).

We should acknowledge that most people are unaware of the internal processes that are active within them and cannot give sensible reports of what governs their learning (Nisbett and Wilson, 1977). The stages of description and attending to feelings are not intended to raise individuals' awarenesses of their own processes, although this may occur to a limited extent, but rather to draw attention to the role that these processes play in experiential learning and what individuals need to be able to do to manage their own reflective activities.

Stage 3 Re-evaluating Experience
It might seem that this third stage, re-evaluating experience, should follow more closely on the learning experience itself. Surely it is natural to move straight from the experience to its evaluation? We have suggested two steps in between: returning to experience and attending to feelings. It is easy to jump from the initial experience to evaluation and judgements are often a part of the original experience. However, we suggest that, except in the special case of insights, it is usually not profitable to do so as we can potentially lose a great deal of value. We may find ourselves operating on false assumptions or reflecting on information which we have not comprehended sufficiently. Attention to description and feelings does not guarantee against this but it can help to minimize the possibility of it occurring.

We now proceed to examine some of the elements of the process of re-evaluation. We have distinguished four aspects which may need to be considered. These we believe can contribute to reflection and enhance its outcomes. They are: first, association, that is, relating of new data to that which is already known; integration, which is seeking relationships among the data; validation to determine the authenticity of the ideas and feelings which have resulted; and appropriation, that is, making knowledge one's own. These aspects should not be thought of as stages through which learners should pass, but elements of a whole. However, some elements would tend to follow others.

All of these stages are influenced by the intent of the learner. As learners, we do not wish to subject all of our experiences to the same level of reflective analysis. Indeed, there are some events in our lives which we would prefer to forget and others that we would like to cherish as simple memories. When we do desire to process our experience and to extract consciously some learning outcomes from it, the way in which we do so will be influenced by our goals and intentions. In many cases our intentions will be quite clear especially when we are involved in a formal learning task and these will guide both our experience and our forms of reflection. In others our intentions may be hazy and ill-defined and only become apparent to us as we proceed. Under these latter conditions close description becomes particularly important. We need to consider then what the experience has to offer to us as we are not able to select those aspects that are directly relevant to our purpose.

ASSOCIATION

Association is the connecting of the ideas and feelings which are part of the original experience and those which have occurred during reflection with existing knowledge and attitudes. It is necessary that the new ideas and information be related to, or associated with, those elements of the pre-existing knowledge relevant to it. Many learning theorists (eg Ausubel, Bruner), particularly those from the information processing school (Lindsay and Norman, 1972), regard this linking of new conceptions to our existing cognitive structure as one of the central features of the learning process.

New associations are facilitated by positive attitudes and a responsive state. The new input linked with our existing knowledge and feelings can challenge us both intellectually and affectively. This aspect of reflection can lead us to the discovery that our old attitudes are no longer consistent with new ideas and feelings, that re-assessment is necessary and, in the cognitive area, that our earlier knowledge needs modifying to accommodate new ideas. It is useful that as many associations be made as possible. Often it happens that an obvious connection sets us reflecting in a particular area with the result that we do not recognize or we neglect other, potentially more fruitful, associations. Immediate associations might not be the most profitable and might only pursue a well-worn path which does not lead to new conceptions. It is well known that many creative leaps in the sciences have occurred through previously unrecognized associations, but this process is also relevant in the more modest learning tasks which face all of us.

There are techniques which can assist us at this stage and help us ensure that we take time to search out those aspects of our prior knowledge and the new experience which may fruitfully be linked. The most common of these is the classic psychoanalytic technique of free association whereby we suspend our rational and analytical judgements and allow ourselves to explore freely whatever associations, whether images, thoughts or feelings, pass through our mind. We can do this in writing, through drawings, on tape, to another person or in whatever way seems to be the least constricting at the time. Rainer (1980) discusses a number of other approaches through writing which can be used. In groups working on similar problems this can be done through the technique of brainstorming (Osborn, 1953; Davies, 1971) in which ideas are generated without criticism, evaluation or comment prior to subsequent appraisal. The greater the number of associations which can be generated at this stage the greater will be the potential for integration.

INTEGRATION

Associations need to be processed to examine whether they are meaningful and useful to us. If they can be integrated into a new whole, a new pattern of ideas and attitudes develops. Association brings together ideas and feelings in an almost|indiscriminate manner; integration begins the process of discrimination. There are two aspects to integration. The first of these is seeking the nature of relationships that have been observed through association. The second is drawing conclusions and arriving at insights into the material which we are processing. Synthesis is the characteristic of this integration phase in which we seek insight, which is the basis for further reflective activity. Boyd and Fales designate this phase as 'resolution':

> The individual experiences a 'coming together' or creative synthesis of various bits of the information previously taken in, and the formation of a new 'solution' or change in the self — what might be called a new gestalt. (Boyd and Fales, 1983, p110)

The methods which can be adopted to assist us in this phase depend on our circumstances, the particular issues we are considering and our preferences. The generation of brain-patterns (Buzan, 1982), concept maps (Novak, 1977), or Venn diagrams (White, 1982) may be useful when dealing with complex cognitive material. These involve portraying visually the links, interconnections and overlaps between ideas, concepts, and phrases. They provide a way to assist us to clarify our thoughts by writing them down and making connections between the perhaps disparate bits of knowledge we have so that we can visualize relationships between them. In areas of knowledge which do not lend themselves to visualization in this way, the use of analogies, similes and metaphors is more appropriate. In the domain of interpersonal relationships repertory grids have been extensively used to help individuals to identify their perceptions and constructions of others who affect them in their lives (see, for example, Chapter 7).

VALIDATION

In validation we are subjecting what we have started to integrate to what we might call 'reality tests'. We are testing for internal consistency between our new appreciations and our existing knowledge and beliefs, for consistency between these and parallel data from others and trying out our new perceptions in new situations. If any contradictions present themselves we have to reappraise the situation and decide on what basis we should proceed. The results from these tests of truth or worth are not necessarily right or wrong. Just because a new perception is not consistent with that held by others it does not necessarily imply that we should reject our own. The idea may be breaking new ground and there will be little to contradict it or we may wish to hold a certain position regardless of conventional wisdom.

One of the techniques which can aid in validation is rehearsal. This can help us relate the knowledge which we believe we have integrated to its applications in our lives. It can take place internally or through literal enactment. At the simplest level we might think through the stages involved in putting our plan into practice. This can be quite a demanding activity which places great weight on concentration and discipline. It can be aided by making written notes, or through a more systematic form of mental rehearsal based on guided imagery. In guided imagery the learner is led by another through a series of steps which require the learner to visualize in detail all the steps required to enact the plan which is being pursued: who will be involved, what will be said, what will be written, what actions follow, what responses will be made, what will upset it and how distractions will be dealt with. As we visualize what might happen, we can correct discrepancies which might emerge and reorient our plans accordingly. This can give us confidence that our plan is capable of being implemented. Guided imagery requires no overt response on the part of the learner, but in some situations where action of a complex or interpersonal kind is required it is useful to rehearse it through various simulations and role-playing activities. These usually require someone to facilitate the process (eg van Ments, 1983), but may also be done in leaderless groups (eg Gibbs, 1983).

APPROPRIATION

For some learning tasks it may be quite sufficient for us to have integrated the new knowledge which has arisen from the experience into our own conceptual framework, but in many areas a further step is required. The new information which has been integrated needs to be appropriated in a very personal way if it is to become our own. Some learning can become so related to the self that it enters into our sense of identity and can have a considerable importance and become a significant force in our lives. Significant feelings can come to be attached to this type of learning and any learning experience which touches this area can give rise to strong emotions that may need to be taken into account in future reflection. Tart has analysed this process and comments:

> adding the ego quality to information *radically* alters the way that inform-ation is treated by the system of consciousness as a whole. (Tart, 1975, p130)

Rogers also points to this reality when, in talking of the experiential character of learning, he writes of:

the student who says 'I am discovering – drawing in from outside and making that which is drawn in a real part of me' . . . (Rogers, 1969, p3)

Not all integrated and validated knowledge is appropriated in this fashion.

Appropriated knowledge becomes part of our value system and it is less amenable to change than other knowledge which we accept and work with but do not make our own to the same degree. Such knowledge people will express as their own and they may feel a strong degree of possessiveness about it. It has a special place within our integrated knowledge. This gives it a higher priority and other integrated material may be interpreted in the light of it.

Miller and others refer to this as an holistic approach, a unity of feeling and intellect. Appropriating new ideas and attitudes leads people to experience:

a sense of wholeness; [they] can exercise [their] intuitive and imaginative faculties as well as [their] rational capabilities (Miller, 1976, p5)

which Bettleheim (1971) refers to as 'the informed heart'. We usually cannot predict which learning will become such a central part of ourselves. All that we can hope for is to select those experiences which are significant to us and ensure that we have processed them in the best way that we can find.

OUTCOMES AND ACTION

While reflection is itself an experience (More, 1974) it is not, of course, an end in itself. It has the objective of making us ready for new experience. The outcomes of reflection may include a new way of doing something, the clarification of an issue, the development of a skill or the resolution of a problem. A new cognitive map may emerge, or a new set of ideas may be identified. The changes may be quite small or they may be large. They could involve the development of new perspectives on experience or changes in behaviour. The synthesis, validation and appropriation of knowledge are outcomes as well as being part of the reflective process. New links may be formed between previously isolated themes and the relative strengths of relationships may be assessed. Again, a significant skill in learning may be developed through an understanding of one's own learning style and needs.

Outcomes of an affective nature enable us to continue on to future learning as well as involve changes in our emotional state, our attitudes or sets of values. They could include a positive attitude towards learning in a particular area, greater confidence or assertiveness, or a changed set of priorities. In any given situation it will be difficult to distinguish between cognitive and affective outcomes and, at any point in time, it may not be possible to articulate what has been learned. In the case of the geology student the outcomes of that experience and reflection on it may have been a recognition of the complexity of the field situation and its conflicting personal and intellectual demands, increased skills in the recognition of various rock types, an awareness of the limitations of underground mapping in the field, and the identification of problems in delimiting boundaries of strata. The student might develop a negative attitude towards field work after experiencing some of the discomforts, but end up with an enhanced sense of his or her own personal capacity through having engaged in hard physical labour.

Some benefits of reflection may be lost if they are not linked to action. Although some of the outcomes are long term and often intangible, such as the appreciation of a work of art, others are more prosaic and can be consolidated by application. Application and action need not necessarily involve acts which can be observed by others. What is important is that the learner makes a commitment of some kind on the basis of his or her learning. What has been rehearsed must face the test of reality. Action ends the reflective process for the time being. Action can obviously occur at any stage of the learning process and it may itself precipitate a new phase of reflective activity.

Unfortunately translating thoughts and ideas into action is not as straightforward a step as it might appear. Argyris (1976) has reported a study which makes gloomy reading for those interested in changing their own behaviour and in facilitating learning for others. He had developed a theory of experiential learning which emphasized the need for learners to question regularly their assumptions about how they act and the purposes they are pursuing, what he terms 'double-loop learning'. He had designed programmes which aimed to make people aware of the ways in which they act towards others and to help them modify their actions in order to achieve their goals more effectively. In two courses Argyris was successful in training the participants (architecture students and educational administrators) in recognizing the dysfunctional aspects of their own behaviour and in being able to identify what they needed to be able to do in order to respond effectively as double-loop learners. They were, however, unable to put this into practice in role-playing situations. Argyris and others have developed his idea in a number of publications and have identified some things which can be done to overcome the difficulties faced in the study above (Argyris, 1982; Argyris and Schön, 1974, 1978; Heller, 1982). What their work points to is the complexity of the learning process in real situations and the need for both teachers and researchers to acknowledge its complexity. Change is hard won; we can desire to do something and believe that it is possible, but still it is difficult to do. Maintaining a positive attitude towards ourselves as learners is a necessary prerequisite for us to overcome some of the problems that Argyris has identified.

The elements of reflection are not as clearly defined in practice as we have suggested earlier and as they are summarized in Figure 3. We have represented them diagrammatically as an aid to exposition. They do not proceed in a simple linear sequence and they are not independent of each other. We have separated them in order to draw attention to some of the features which we believe are often overlooked by both teachers and

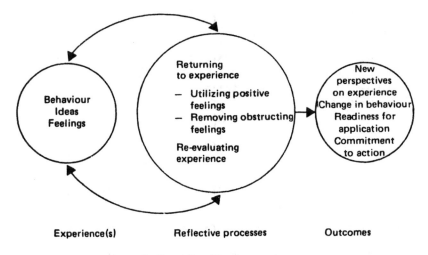

Figure 3 *The reflection process in context*

learners. To do justice to the full complexities of the process would involve
a description which indicated the continual cycling back and forth
between elements, the omission of some stages at times and the
compression of some of the elements we have described. Nevertheless if
learners are having difficulties in reflecting, it can be useful to think about
the stages we have described and examine whether any of them have
been omitted.

Assisting in the Process of Reflection

Most of the examples we have given in the description of stages have
referred to what individuals can do for themselves. However, there are
limits to what each of us can achieve unaided and often the learning
process can be considerably accelerated by appropriate support,
encouragement and intervention by others. Indeed, reflection alone has
many challenges as Habermas recognizes:

> The self-reflection of a lone subject . . . requires a quite paradoxical achieve-
> ment: one part of the self must be split off from the other part in such a
> manner that the subject can be in a position to render aid to itself . . . [further-
> more] in the act of self-reflection the subject can deceive itself. (Habermas,
> 1974, cited in Grundy and Kemmis, 1982, p87)

We believe that if teachers and others assisting learners are to have an
effective role in promoting learning that role is essentially to provide a
stimulus for learning, to support the learner in the process and to assist
the learner in extracting the maximum benefit from what occurs. Those
who plan to set up a learning situation, whether it be formal or informal,
cannot presume that the experience which they hope to elicit will actually
take place. The nature of the experience will be determined largely by
what the learner brings to the situation. Sometimes the outcome is

36

different from what was planned and the teacher can be placed in the unenviable position of attempting to work with an experience which the student did not have. Teachers need to be conscious of the priorities of learners in the process of learning, and need to appreciate that what emerges from the learning activity will be determined more by the learner than by the person who designed the activity.

Susan Knights in Chapter 5 discusses the fundamental importance of a listener in facilitating processes of reflection, but here we wish to indicate the role of others at each of the stages we have described above.

Not only can teachers or facilitators adopt the important listening role but they can also suggest a variety of techniques which may be appropriate at each stage. To provide this assistance the helper need not be in a formal teacher-learner relationship with the learner, substantial benefits can be gained by peer-assisted learning at a formal or informal level (Cornwall, 1979), and from support groups within a profession or institution (Kirschenbaum and Glaser, 1978).

At the initial stage of returning to experience, facilitators can assist the learner to describe as objectively as possible what has taken place in the experience and to help him or her to avoid interpretations and analysis. This is directly analogous to the debriefing procedure for pilots after a mission. The facilitator asks for a detailed account of what happened,draws out events which at first may have gone unnoticed and draws attention to unacknowledged interpretations and speculations. Listening skills are important in this and the facilitator needs a keen awareness of the ways in which learners use language to describe or interpret their situation. It is vital that facilitators offer no interpretations or analyses of their own. Learners themselves can also check out the objectivity of their perceptions with their peers, especially those who have experienced the same event.

In the second stage, attending to feelings, learners can be assisted by being encouraged to be aware of the feelings that were present during the initial experience and to bring these to their consciousness. Because some feelings can be a barrier to learning they need to be clearly understood. Not only do they need to be identified but the learner needs to work with them to understand their significance and to find ways of discharging, transforming or celebrating them. The single most important contribution facilitators can make is to give free and undivided attention to the learner and what Rogers (1961) describes as 'unconditional positive regard'. If facilitators are more experienced and more confident they can also draw the attention of the learner to his or her behaviour: the non-verbal signs which betray emotions, the missing elements of a description and the repetitions which appear to punctuate the recollection. Facilitators should be aware of the limits of their own skill and be prepared to put learners in touch with those people who can assist in a more sophisticated way if needed. The particular approaches which appear to have most to offer at this stage are those which employ techniques such as those used in co-counselling in which learners assist each other, either on a one-to-one basis or in groups. For the unaided learner both writing (Rainer, 1980) and meditative (Heron, 1982) approaches have much to contribute.

At the re-evaluation stages facilitators have perhaps less to offer of their personal resources and need to draw on more of their technical skills than earlier in the process. They become a resource with access to various specialized techniques, but they must continue to offer their support and encouragement. They can help to clarify learners' intentions through the application of competency models (Knowles, 1980), providing criteria for performance, and generally through supportive questioning. They can provide technical assistance through the provision of repertory grids to clarify learners' constructs, through descriptions of free association methods, through leading brainstorming sessions to aid association and through introducing concept maps or the other devices mentioned earlier to aid integration. They can lead guided imagery sessions, initiate role-playing sessions and provide the context for applications.

Generally speaking, the role of those who assist the learner is to provide a context and a space to learn, give support and encouragement, listen to the learner and provide access to particular devices which may be of use. They may also at times act as a sounding board and help the learner clarify intentions and set goals. Of course, all this must be within the context of the learner's needs and interests. They also have roles to stimulate learning and initiate new experiences but these are beyond the scope of our present discussion. Perhaps one of their most important roles is to alert people to the nature of reflection in the learning process and provide ways whereby others can assist it at its various stages.

Conclusions

We have given an account of the reflective process which draws attention to what we regard as some of the areas of learning which have, until recently, been overlooked by researchers and under-emphasized by teachers and trainers. Although we have focused on the individual in this we hope that the implications for group reflection and for more formal learning situations are apparent. Learning theory, despite some hopeful signs, has yet to make any substantial contributions to the kinds of learning tasks with which we are normally faced. However, we hope we have offered some clues which may be pursued by those of us in the education profession.

Much research needs to be conducted in all of the areas we have considered. Many of our remarks cannot be underpinned by the kinds of research we would wish for. To date most research on learning has not sufficiently respected the unique perspective of the learner and has not taken into account the affective dimension to which we have referred. Nevertheless, considerable progress has been made in recent years on clarifying some of the issues involved. The recent book by Dunlop (1984) is helpful in pointing to some of the issues involved in the education of feeling and emotion, and the forms of co-operative inquiry and action research discussed in Chapters 9 and 10 and by Reason and Rowan (1981) who offer ways in which we might be able to conduct research in this area. The importance of reflection in professional practice is beginning to be recognized. The important book, *The Reflective Practitioner*, by Schön (1983), which came to our attention after completing this chapter, offers some useful directions for exploring reflection-in-action. If professionals are to develop skills in reflective thinking it is important that they be encouraged to do so in their initial training. One of us has been investigating the application of one aspect of reflection: self-assessment in courses of education for the professions (Boud and Lublin, 1983a, 1983b).

Many of the ideas introduced here are developed in greater detail in the chapters which follow and examples are given of techniques we have mentioned in passing.

References

Abbs, P (1974) *Autobiography in Education*, London: Heinemann Educational

Argyris, C (1976) Theories of action that inhibit individual learning, *American Psychologist*, 39, pp638-654

Argyris, C (1982) *Reasoning, Learning and Action*, San Francisco: Jossey-Bass

Argyris, C and Schön, D (1974) *Theory into Practice*, San Francisco: Jossey-Bass

Argyris, C and Schön, D (1978) *Organizational Learning: a Theory of Action Perspective*, Reading, Mass: Addison-Wesley

Bettleheim, B (1971) *The Informed Heart*, New York: Avon

Boud, D J and Lublin, J R (1983a) Student self-assessment, in Squires, G (ed) *Innovation through Recession*, Guildford: Society for Research into Higher Education, pp93-99

Boud, D J and Lublin, J R (1983b) *Self Assessment in Professional Education*, Report to the Education Research and Development Committee, Tertiary Education Research Centre, University of New South Wales

Boud, D and Pascoe, J (1978) What is experiential learning? and Conceptualizing experiential education, in Boud, D and Pascoe, J (eds) *Experiential Learning: Developments in Australian Post-Secondary Education*, Sydney: Australian Consortium on Experiential Education, pp1-6, 61-64

Boyd, E M and Fales, A W (1983) Reflective learning: key to learning from experience, *Journal of Humanistic Psychology*, 23, 2, pp99-117

Buzan, T (1982) *Use Your Head*, London: British Broadcasting Corporation, Revised Edition

Coleman, J C (1976) Differences between experiential and classroom learning, in Keeton, M (ed) *Experiential Learning: Rationale, Characteristics and Assessment*, San Francisco: Jossey-Bass, pp49-61

Cornwall, M G (1979) *Students as Teachers: Peer Teaching in Higher Education*, Cowo-Publicatie 7906-01, Amsterdam: University of Amsterdam

Cunningham, P M (1983) Helping students extract meaning from experience, *New Directions for Continuing Education*, 19, pp57-69

Davies, I K (1971) *The Management of Learning*, London: McGraw-Hill

Dewey, J (1916) *Democracy in Education*, New York: Macmillan

Dewey, J (1933) *How We Think*, Boston: D C Heath, Revised Edition

Dunlop, F (1984) *The Education of Feeling and Emotion*, London: George Allen and Unwin

Entwistle, N and Ramsden, P (1983) *Understanding Student Learning*, London: Croom Helm

Freire, P (1970) *Pedagogy of the Oppressed*, London: Penguin

Gibbs, G (1983) Using role plays in interpersonal skills training: a peer learning approach, *Simulation/Games for Learning*, 13, 4, pp147-155

Gibbs, G, Morgan, A and Taylor, E (1982) A review of the research of Ference Marton and the Goteborg Group: a phenomenological research perspective on learning, *Higher Education*, 11, pp123-145

Grundy, S and Kemmis, S (1982) Educational action research in Australia: the state of the art (an overview), in Kemmis, S et al (eds) *The Action Research Reader*, Waurn Ponds, Victoria: Deakin University

Habermas, J (1974) *Theory and Practice*, London: Heinemann

Heller, J F (1982) *Increasing Faculty and Administrative Effectiveness*, San Francisco: Jossey-Bass

Heron, J (1982) Education of the affect: the unexplored domain, in Habershaw, T (ed) *Three Ways to Learn*, Preston: Standing Conference on Educational Development Services in Polytechnics pp31-46

Kelly, G A (1955) *The Psychology of Personal Constructs, 1 and 2*, New York: Norton

Kirschenbaum, H and Glaser, B (1978) *Developing Support Groups*, La Jolla, California: University Associates

Knapper, C K and Cropley, A J (in press) *Lifelong Learning and Higher Education*, London: Croom Helm

Knowles, M S (1980) *The Modern Practice of Adult Education*, Chicago: Follet, Revised Edition

Lindsay, P H and Norman, D A (1972) *Human Information Processing*, New York: Academic Press

Mezirow, J (1978) *Education for Perspective Transformation: Women's Reentry Programs in Community Colleges*, New York: Centre for Adult Education, Columbia University

Mezirow, J (1981) A critical theory of adult learning and education, *Adult Education*, 32, 1, pp3-24

Miller, J P (1976) *Humanizing the Classroom: Models of Teaching in Affective Education*, New York: Praeger Publishers

More, W S (1974) *Emotions and Adult Learning*, Farnborough: Saxon House

Nisbett, R E and Wilson, D W (1977) Telling more than we can know: verbal reports on mental processes, *Psychological Review*, 84, 3, pp231-259

Novak, J D (1977) *A Theory of Education*, Ithaca: Cornell University Press

Osborn, A F (1953) *Applied Imagination*, New York: Scribner

Rainer, T (1980) *The New Diary*, London: Angus and Robertson

Reason, P and Rowan, J (eds) (1981) *Human Inquiry: A Source Book of New Paradigm Research*, Chichester: John Wiley

Reed, D (1981) *Education for a People's Movement*, Boston: South End Press

Rogers, C R (1961) *On Becoming a Person*, Boston: Houghton Mifflin

Rogers, C R (1969) *Freedom to Learn*, Columbus, Ohio: Merrill

Säljö, R (1981) Learning approach and outcome: some empirical observations, *Instructional Science*, 10, pp47-65

Schön, D A (1983) *The Reflective Practitioner: How Professionals Think in Action*, London: Temple Smith

Tart, C T (1975) *States of Consciousness*, New York: E P Dutton

Taylor, M (1981) The social dimensions of adult learning, in Salter, L (ed) *Communication Studies in Canada*, Toronto: Butterworths, pp133-146

Tough, A (1979) *The Adult's Learning Projects*, Toronto: Ontario Institute for Studies in Education, Second Edition

Van Manen, M (1977) Linking ways of knowing with ways of being practical, *Curriculum Inquiry*, 6, 2, pp205-228

van Ments, M (1983) *The Effective Use of Role-Play*, London: Kogan Page

White, R T (1982) Two lessons in one: what you taught and what they learned in science, *Set: Research Information for Teachers*, 1, item 7

Zeichner, K M (1982) Reflective teaching and field-based experience in teacher education, *Interchange*, 12, 4, pp1-22

CHAPTER 2
Autobiographical Learning

J P Powell, *University of New South Wales*

Most people who keep personal journals or diaries or who publish their autobiographies usually do not do so in order to discover truths about themselves or to make a more general contribution to our understanding of the nature of human learning (Pascal, 1960). The creation and use of such documents can be undertaken, however, solely for such purposes and it is with these we shall be concerned here. Since 1976 I have been teaching a course dealing with the nature of adult learning. During that period I have become progressively more involved with working out ways in which we can gain access to prior learning experiences in order to derive insights from them which will assist us in coming to terms with our own approaches to learning and, more generally, in developing our understanding of the immensely complex dynamic relationship between teaching and learning. These are topics which are full of interest from an intellectual viewpoint and of profound importance educationally. I must confess, however, after grappling with them for eight years, that they are also very resistant to theoretical analysis and full of problems for the teacher. In order to set what follows in a context, it will be helpful to begin by briefly surveying the rather sparse literature in order to indicate some of the research and teaching applications of autobiographical material.

Before doing so, however, mention should also be made of another major area of human endeavour which, although neglected by educational researchers, has much to say to us about the role of reflective thought in adult learning. I refer here to the broad and varied domain of the performing arts and craft skills. Learning in this area crucially depends upon self-observation and a close knowledge of the difference between one's current performance and the achievements which are required if progress is to be made. An important contribution to our understanding of this topic has recently been made by Howard (1982) in a work which combines philosophical, psychological and educational considerations with the perspective of a practising artist.

Use of Life Histories

Research workers in the social sciences have for some time made use of a range of personal documents in order to throw light on a wide variety of problems. Allport (1942) discussed the value of autobiographies, letters, diaries and literary works as a means of studying religious experiences, adolescence, and creativity. Jung (1972) has reviewed studies of personality development, conducted in the 1920s and 1930s, based upon student autobiographies. Anthropologists have made extensive use of life histories in order to present details of cultures other than their own (Langness, 1965; Langness and Frank, 1981; Strathern, 1979). Historians have relied heavily upon the autobiographies and diaries of well-known figures and more recently have been exploring oral history (Blythe, 1972) and written accounts of their lives produced by 'ordinary folk' (Burnett, 1974, 1982). An increasing number of the latter are now being made more widely available by publishers (Haggard, 1982; Edwards, 1982).

Educators have been rather slow to see the potential of autobiographical material and other personal reports on learning. There have been some attempts to collect individual reflections on learning for course evaluation purposes (Duke, 1977; Warren, 1981) and some exploratory studies have been conducted of the longer-term impact of education (Nier, 1979; Powell, 1983; Thielens, 1977). A daunting mass of published autobiographical material is available to researchers willing to sift through it for evidence of the effects of education upon the lives of individuals, and further information could be derived from an analysis of *Festschriften* and accounts by graduates of the impact upon them of university teachers (Epstein, 1981). Finally, there is the work of Pinar and Grumet (1976) which seeks to develop a fresh perspective on the curriculum based upon reconstructions of educational experience from the viewpoint of the learner rather than that of the teacher or the system.

Educational practitioners who have employed personal documents as tools for learning have either asked students to keep some form of diary in which to record learning activities as they occurred (Christensen, 1981; French, 1976; Hettich, 1976; Ingram, 1979) or have encouraged the creation of wider-ranging accounts of earlier educational experiences which are then explored in order to prepare for future life events. The latter appear to have featured most often in professional preparation programmes for teachers (Abbs, 1974; Dow, 1979).

These developments in the practice of teaching and research have drawn upon an intellectual tradition which is radically different from the reductionist behaviourism which has characterized, until quite recently, much of our thinking about education. This tradition relies upon ideas drawn from phenomenology, psychoanalysis, existentialism, and humanistic psychology, rather than upon, for example, the theory and practice of behaviour modification. Above all, perhaps, it seeks to give contemporary form to the ancient art of hermeneutics (Howard, 1983), that is, the gradual penetration of the meaning of text through progressive refinements of interpretation. The aim is to reveal, describe, and interpret the past experience of individuals in order to illuminate the present and make manifest the potentialities of the future. Pinar and Grumet put it this way:

we might say that we are educated to the extent that we are conscious of
our experience and to the degree that we are freed by this knowledge to act
through skills required to transform our world. (Pinar and Grumer, 1976, p38)

We can now turn to three illustrations of the use of autobiographical
material for teaching purposes. Abbs is a persuasive advocate of the value
of such accounts in the training of teachers: 'Who is better equipped to
bring education alive than one who knows through his inmost experience
what education is?' (p6) He describes what he has in mind as follows:

The discipline of autobiography which I am advocating is primarily an inward
and creative discipline centred on the related acts of reflecting on and recreating the personal past. It is not academic. It begins and ends with what is
given to experience. (Abbs, 1974, pp12-13)

He suggests that for the method to succeed groups of not more than
12 students should meet for an hour each week for at least ten weeks.
During this period of time each student works at creating a written
account of his or her educational experience and the weekly meetings are
used to enable each person to read a passage from his or her autobiography
so that it can be supportively commented upon by peers and the teacher.
The aim is to encourage the progressive reconstruction of experience
without imposing any restraints upon the student's choice of the content
and manner of writing. The bulk of Abbs' book consists of extended
extracts from students' work.

The second example is a course called 'Education through
Autobiography' in the Open University E200 series (Barnes, 1981). The
aim of this course is to help students construct their own educational
autobiography as an aid to understanding the range of experiences which
contribute to an individual's development. The course text essentially
consists of 134 questions, extensively illustrated with quotations from
Edward Blishen's *Sorry, Dad*, designed to facilitate recollection of and
reflection upon encounters with educational institutions.

The final example is drawn from the work of Pinar and Grumet (1976)
which I shall present in a little more detail, partly because they have
described their approach at some length and partly because the opaqueness
of their style makes it difficult for the reader to feel confident that their
meaning has been correctly grasped. Their general theoretical position,
and their recommendations for practice, appear to be a reaction against
what they see as the failure of most educational research to focus upon
the experience of learning viewed from the perspective of the student.
They urge the necessity to move away from the study of the external
curriculum, towards a focus upon the inner reality of the educational
experiences of individual learners.

The method proposed to achieve this is termed *currere* and it consists
of the following procedural stages. First, a recapturing of past educational
experiences without any attempt at interpretation; second, an anticipation
through free association of ideas of the future development of the
individual's current intellectual interests; third, a description of current
interests and feelings about them; and finally, a synthesis of these three

43

sets of data. The aim is to illuminate the present and future rather than events of the past: an orientation similar to that of Abbs and the Open University course.

> We are . . . less interested in autobiography as a record of a student's passage through schooling, as a souvenir of the trip, than as a source of energy and direction for the journey. (Pinar and Grumet, 1976, p111)

Students are asked to write essays and diary entries, some of which are then subjected to critical analysis by peers or the teacher (the 'respondents') and are then rewritten with the student being encouraged to adopt a distancing technique in order to become a self-respondent. Elsewhere Grumet (1981) gives a brief outline of the procedure employed in one of their courses at the University of Rochester. Students are asked to write an essay consisting of three narratives self-categorized as educational experiences. This text is then subjected to analysis and interpretation intended to expose the extent to which it fails to match reality. The student then reconstructs the text in the light of these comments.

As I have indicated, Abbs' book largely consists of the products of his teaching method and the work of Pinar and Grumet is mainly comprised of the theoretical and ideological underpinnings of their pedagogic practice. In neither case is very much assistance offered to those who might wish to use autobiographical materials in their own teaching. The Open University course is a special case, not only because it is part of a distance education programme, but because whatever the students write is not made available either to peers or teachers. This gives me a good excuse to report on my own practice in rather more detail.

Explorations in Personal Learning

I chose this title for the course in an attempt to make plain that it would not be dealing with the kinds of topic commonly to be found in textbooks dealing with learning. The focus of the course was the nature of adult learning as experienced by the learner and the students were postgraduates who were engaged in the teaching of medical or paramedical training programmes. The procedure was to encourage reflection upon classroom events in a small group setting in order to identify, and consider the implications of, factors which helped or hindered learning (Powell, 1977, 1980, 1981a, 1981b).

I should point out that, with the exception of the book by Abbs, I have only recently become acquainted with the authors whose work I have mentioned earlier. My own practice, like that of the great majority of teachers, was not derived from any carefully devised theoretical position, but was based upon beliefs and insights which had emerged in a very *ad hoc* and leisurely manner over a number of years of experience of trying to assist others to learn. I operated with hunches about what might work and did not hesitate to modify or abandon procedures which proved to be unsuccessful as means to achieving my educational purposes.

In order to encourage students to reflect upon their own learning

a variety of techniques was used as it became clear that this was a far
more problematical activity than I had at first supposed. Working in pairs,
one student tackled a problem while the other observed: they then
discussed the manner in which the problem had been approached. At the
end of each class every student completed a 'reflections sheet' which asked
them to identify what they had learnt, comment on any emotional
reactions, and list any factors which had helped or hindered their learning.
During each class I interrupted the proceedings from time to time in order
to comment upon an event which might have implications for learning;
students were invited to say how they viewed the event and how they felt
about it. I also gave accounts each week, in writing, of my view of the
progress of the course and encouraged students to respond to these by
offering their own impressions from the perspective of the learner. At the
end of the course each student wrote a substantial evaluation of it centred
upon its impact on their own learning, and the final class meeting was
devoted to a discussion of the entire course. A complete videotape record
was made of the course during the second time it was taught, the idea
being to make use of some of this material to stimulate reflection upon
what was happening: none of this tape was ever replayed. Finally, a
colleague acted as a participant observer each time the course was taught,
and immediately after each class the teacher was able to reflect upon what
had happened with the aid of a debriefing interview (see Powell and
Shanker, 1982).

Until now I had not appreciated the extent and variety of the techniques
which were employed — not all of these were used every time — to
facilitate reflective activity by students and teacher. Some students, of
their own accord, also kept a diary to serve as an *aide-mémoire* when
the time came to write the course evaluation. Despite this rather
overwhelming battery of devices I came to feel that, on the whole, they
were more productive for the teacher than for the learners whom they
were designed to assist. I learnt a great deal about myself as a teacher and
developed my skills in analysing the dynamics of teaching and learning
and identifying significant features of learning environments, but became
increasingly dissatisfied with the extent to which the students were
learning. As I have pointed out elsewhere (Powell, 1981b), there is
something bizarre about teachers learning more than students.

The content of this course consisted almost entirely of reflections
about one's own learning and that of others and I seriously underestimated
the problems which this would pose for students. It is extraordinarily
difficult to identify what one is learning when engaged in a learning task
or at a time quite close to that period of activity: try to identify
something which you learnt today! It is much easier to report when
learning is not taking place or to describe one's feelings about what is
happening. At least part of the difficulty lies in the intellectual demand
imposed by the sudden switching of attention which is required for
immediate reflection on learning. One has to be able to move rapidly
and with ease from, say, intense involvement in a discussion of a

substantive point to a meta-discussion of ideas and feelings quite unrelated to what was being talked about a short time before. I do not find this an easy task to manage despite having had the benefit of 70 hours of practice in the debriefing sessions. The distancing which is required and the cognitive dislocation which is involved created major problems for many students and limited what they were able to gain from the course. I attempted to overcome this by introducing a break in the middle of each two-hour class and devoting the second half to analysing and interpreting what took place in the first half, but this did not improve matters to the extent I had anticipated because there was still a strong tendency for the discussion to return to issues which had been raised prior to the break.

Another explanation for the difficulties experienced by the students may lie in the nature of what they were being asked to reflect upon. If the learning task consists of memorizing factual material or acquiring a manipulative skill such as how to operate a capstan lathe then it is not too difficult to identify what is being learnt and the extent of the progress being made. In this case, however, much of the content of what was to be learnt was far more elusive and often involved almost imperceptible changes in the learner which required a considerable period of time to become apparent to an introspective subject or to observers. Examples of such changes would be modification of attitudes towards teaching and learning, displacement of well-entrenched beliefs, emergence of alternative conceptions of the teacher's role, adoption of unfamiliar perspectives on adult learning, and adjustments to value systems. Even if some learning is taking place in these areas it seems most unlikely that we could recognize this to be the case at the time. This is not to deny, of course, that quite dramatic changes can occur in individuals, of the kind Saint Paul experienced on the road to Damascus, as a consequence of a sudden insight or quite brief experience, but these seem to be rare, especially in educational settings.

Techniques to Aid Reflection

The 'reflection sheets' which were completed at the end of each class were devices for encouraging students to stand back from what they had been doing and think about what it meant for their own learning and what it entailed for their work as teachers of others. Most found this a difficult task to complete and I was often disappointed with the results. Perhaps I expected too much from a brief activity usually undertaken in some haste. There is also a need to be cautious in assuming that the written comments accurately represent the extent of the reflective thinking which the task may have prompted.

As opportunity offered I would make remarks on classroom events in order to encourage thoughts about their implications for teaching and learning and elicit comments concerned with their impact on individuals. For example, I might refer to the absence of one student and the effect this had on interaction in the group, or to my own feelings about a remark which I took to be critical of myself, or to the effects of a period of silence, or to changes in seating positions. The aim was to sharpen analytical and observational powers and, by example, promote reflection upon what was happening in class and its implications for learning. Sometimes these comments led to valuable discussion but often they appeared to be viewed as interruptions to the consideration of whatever topic had been in view immediately beforehand. It was impossible to identify any pattern to the responses and when they proved unfruitful, I attributed this to problems associated with reflexive thinking which have already been mentioned.

In a final attempt to overcome these I decided to require everyone, during the early weeks of the course, to write an autobiographical account of their own encounters with educational institutions which attempted to identify learning experiences which had, in retrospect, proved to be of particular significance. Each autobiography was photocopied and distributed to each student and the course was substantially redesigned so that the first half of each meeting was devoted to a discussion of one student's story and the second half, as before, to an analysis of what took place during the first half.

This resolved several problems in the design of the course by giving a sharper focus to class discussions. To get things started I wrote my own account which was considered in the second meeting. I found it quite easy to write about three pages but to get beyond that far more effort was required. Few students wrote at greater length: perhaps they were following the example I had set! It seems likely, however, that the production of more substantial accounts demands extended recollection and progressive expansion of the material over a considerable period of time. No attempt was made to do this although there can be little doubt that it would be educationally valuable to construct an entire course, as suggested by Abbs, around the creation of an autobiography. I was too attached to the value of discussing classroom events to wish to do this.

Several of the accounts included comments on what was involved in reconstructing the educational past and one student provided a quite detailed picture of his way of doing this:

> During the last four days I have examined my memories of my days at school and university. On the first occasion a few outstanding memories, which I have never really lost, came readily to the surface. Feelings and pictures appeared — many of events outside the educational system, but others firmly rooted in my educational past. During the last four days more and more of such memories appeared . . . even solid chunks of content, particularly in subjects of which I had been particularly fond. By the time I sat down to write I found that events that I had remembered early in the week I had temporarily forgotten, but I had a host of new and probably important educational memories. I have a feeling that given enough time . . . I could build up a few pages of educational memories that would be quite different from those which I will write on this occasion.

The autobiographies constituted a very diverse and rich set of materials and although there is not space here to display the range of their content a few extracts will show the ease with which they could be used to trigger discussion of important educational issues.

> I have little doubt that what respect for learning and scholarship I now have derived greatly from my close contact with an outstanding teacher . . . the devotion and seriousness with which he encouraged us all to attend to our studies was a deep and lasting influence.

> I'll be forever thankful to a teacher there who believed that children should enjoy and learn from books and reading . . . He used to read from a novel each day and enrolled us all in the local junior library.

> We used to model with clay . . . I remember very clearly the ritual for putting the clay away afterwards! It was very important to stand with our toes in line with the row of nails in the floorboards . . . One morning I climbed out onto the window ledge and heard the teacher call out 'Ah, you're on the window ledge. You're different to the other children are you?' The embarrassment and hurt still burn my senses.

> I can recall no attempt to elicit creative thinking, or even to acknowledge individual differences in this class of fifty children. I learnt conformity to authority, to conceal feeling and to develop a protective similarity to my peers.

> An outstanding teacher encouraged me to think. I liked the way he used open-ended questions and then sought to encourage me to explain why I had made the deduction I had. He always sought to encourage me to consider other angles and reflect.

> Most staff members were remote, highly intelligent, cold, studious individuals centred on themselves.

> Not one lecturer in first-year appeared interested in anything other than getting through his material at as fast a rate as possible. I failed three subjects out of four.

> Biochemistry was made difficult by the lecturer. He lectured with his back to the audience, chalk in his right hand, eraser in his left, scribbling complex equations which were as rapidly erased.

> The final examinations went on for six weeks and were a tremendous test of fortitude. I had nightmares about them for many years.

> Looking back, it's the personality of my teachers that was most significant to me. The professor who seemed so human and urbane, and my tutor who spoke quietly, dressed well and treated everyone with respect. I modelled myself after them both, and I still find parts of them in me.

Remarks on Methods

It is important to make clear at the beginning the purpose and nature of the writing task in which students are to engage. It can be helpful to ask everyone to read an example of autobiographical writing which deals with those aspects of educational experience that are of particular relevance to the course. Given the very limited amount of time which will be available for writing and discussion it is essential to assist students to focus quite sharply upon recollections which bear upon current learning, future professional practice or whatever else constitutes the content of the course. This focus can be selected from a wide range of options: family life, non-formal learning, primary schooling, higher education, working life or vacation jobs, leisure activities, or events perceived as being especially formative or significant. Without clear guidance on the nature of the focus of recollection the written accounts are likely to exhibit so much diversity that discussion of them will prove an unnecessarily difficult and possibly unproductive task.

Given the highly personal nature of this mode of expression it is also important for students to have the freedom to determine the extent of self-disclosure. If nobody but the author is to have access to the autobiography, as with the assignment for the Open University course mentioned earlier, then it seems likely that the content will be somewhat different from that which will be contained in a more public document. If the accounts are to be read by others, and especially if they are to be discussed in class, then the teacher has a responsibility to create a climate of trust which respects each individual's contribution. The need for this is stressed by Abbs:

> Here the tutor's influence must be subtle and indirect. Any compulsion is alien to the spirit of autobiography. By his presence the tutor must be able to create the feel of trust: that trust in which each student feels able to present himself, to be what he is. (Abbs, 1974, p22)

Pinar and Grumet also comment on this point:

> I was careful in my response to their writing. I did not write comments upon their papers, preferring to number the sentences on a separate sheet of paper. I wanted my response to provide a dialogic view, but not a judgemental one. (Pinar and Grumet, 1976, p155)

Brief autobiographies take an enormous amount for granted which is quite unfamiliar to the reader and this tends to lead to a large number of responses which are clarificatory questions. Sometimes these questions prompted the recall of further details and resulted in the exploration of topics which were hidden in the written narrative, but at other times they were less fruitful.

Reconstructions of educational experience enable students to get to know far more about their peers and teachers than would commonly be the case, and many students commented upon the value of this. They do not, however, guarantee that class discussion will be lively and productive. At times the quality of discussion was constrained by our inability to exploit the potential of one of the accounts. This may have been because its content was somewhat conventional or its expression cautious, or because we could not readily relate it to our own experience. As Sherlock Holmes observed: 'The more featureless and commonplace a crime is, the more difficult it is to bring it home.' In such cases it was usually difficult to get the discussion moving and this could be an embarrassment to the author and thus to everyone else. One method of avoiding this is to ask the writer to begin by presenting recollections which have come to mind since the account was completed and by inviting comments on particular topics.

These are only minor reservations to make about the use of

autobiographical method. I am convinced of its value as a technique for encouraging students to explore the nature of their own learning experiences and thus deepen their understanding of themselves as learners. For those who are preparing for or engaged in the profession of teaching, the reconstruction of educational history offers rich opportunities for gaining insights into the nature of teaching and learning and the effects of the environment in which these activities take place.

As I have indicated here, my own attempts to help students to become more reflective about what they do as learners have been characterized by frequent changes in technique and course design. I have always felt frustrated by and dissatisfied with what I saw as my very limited achievements in what I believe to be one of the key areas of adult learning. Each year I begin with a vision of an ideal course, perfect students and an omnicompetent teacher. Unfortunately, it never works out that way — hence the constant changes in approach in a vain attempt to close the gap between ideal and reality. Writing this account of what I have been doing has helped me to realize the need to guard against the folly of unrealistic expectations: 'If only the students were different and I were more skilful!' By its very nature the act of reflection can only reveal what we are.

References

Abbs, P (1974) *Autobiography in Education*, London: Heinemann

Allport, G W (1942) *The Use of Personal Documents in Psychological Science*, New York: Social Science Research Council

Barnes, P (1981) *Education through Autobiography*, Milton Keynes: Open University Press

Blythe, R (1972) *Akenfield*, Harmondsworth: Penguin

Burnett, J (1974) *Useful Toil: Autobiographies of Working People from the 1820s to the 1920s*, London: Allen Lane

Burnett, J (1982) *Destiny Obscure: Autobiographies of Childhood, Education and Family from the 1820s to the 1920s*, London: Allen Lane

Christensen, R S (1981) 'Dear diary': a learning tool for adults, *Lifelong Learning: the Adult Years*, 5, 2, pp4-5 and 31

Dow, G M (1979) *Learning to Teach, Teaching to Learn*, London: Routledge & Kegan Paul

Duke, D L (1977) Debriefing: a tool for curriculum research and course improvement, *Journal of Curriculum Studies*, 9, pp157-163

Edwards, G B (1982) *The Book of Ebenezer le Page*, Harmondsworth: Penguin

Epstein, J (ed) (1981) *Masters: Portraits of Great Teachers*, New York: Basic Books

French, D (1976) History 213 or the yearning to be free, *Liberal Education*, 62, pp472-487

Grumet, M R (1981) Restitution and reconstruction of educational experience: an autobiographical method for curriculum theory, in Lawn, M and Barton, L (eds) *Rethinking Curriculum Studies*, London: Croom Helm

Haggard, L R (ed) (1982) *I Walked by Night, being the Life and History of the King of the Norfolk Poachers*, Oxford: Oxford University Press

Hettich, P (1976) The journal: an autobiographical approach to learning, *Teaching of Psychology*, 3, pp60-63

Howard, R J (1983) *Three Faces of Hermeneutics*, Berkeley: University of California Press

Howard, V A (1982) *Artistry: the Work of Artists*, Indianapolis: Hackett Publishing

Ingram, L C (1979) Teaching the sociology of religion: the student's religious autobiography, *Teaching Sociology*, 6, pp161-172

Jung, J (1972) Autobiographies of college students as a teaching and research tool in the study of personality development, *American Psychologist*, 27, pp779-783

Langness, J L (1965) *The Life History in Anthropological Science*, New York: Holt, Rinehart and Winston

Langness, L L and Frank, G (1981) *Lives: An Anthropological Approach to Biography*, Novato, Calif: Sharp Publishers

Nier, C J (1979) Educational autobiographies: explorations of affective impact, *Teacher Education*, 15, pp14-20

Pascal, R (1960) *Design and Truth in Autobiography*, London: Routledge & Kegan Paul

Pinar, W F and Grumet, M R (1976) *Toward a Poor Curriculum*, Dubuque, Iowa: Kendall/Hunt Publishing

Powell, J P (1977) Tertiary teachers learning about learning, *R & D Paper*, No 50, Sydney: Tertiary Education Research Centre, University of New South Wales

Powell, J P (1980) Freedom to learn: designing courses for students rather than teachers, in Miller, A H (ed) *Research and Development in Higher Education*, Vol 3. Sydney: HERDSA

Powell, J P (1981a) Helping and hindering learning, *Higher Education*, 10, pp103-117

Powell, J P (1981b) Reducing teacher control, in Boud, D (ed) *Developing Student Autonomy in Learning*, London: Kogan Page

Powell, J P (1983) The impact of higher education: graduates report on what they learnt, in Moses, I (ed) *Research and Development in Higher Education*, Vol 6, Sydney: HERDSA

Powell, J P and Shanker, V S (1982) The course planning and monitoring activities of a university teacher, *Higher Education*, 11, pp289-301

Strathern, A [trans] (1979) *Ongka: A Self-account by a New Guinea Big-man*, London: Duckworth

Thielens, W (1977) Undergraduate definitions of learning from teachers, *Sociology of Education*, 50, pp159-181

Warren, C (1981) Using the written life history for programme evaluation, *Canadian Journal of University Continuing Education*, 7, No 2, pp10-14

CHAPTER 3
Writing and Reflection

David Walker, *Educational Centre, Sydney*

Introduction

There is a growing interest in the role of writing in learning, and a corresponding interest in finding ways that both teachers and learners can use to incorporate writing more effectively into learning experiences. The aim of this chapter is to encourage and assist readers to make use of writing as an aid to reflection. The chapter will outline a method of writing that I have worked with over the last three years. It will include conclusions which both my students and I have drawn from this experience, and some practical advice on how to use writing as a tool to foster reflection.

There are many uses of writing currently being proposed. The different names applied to them capture something of their diversity. There are journals, diaries, record books, portfolios, verbatims, sociological diaries, dossiers and logs. What all these have in common is that they are using writing in the service of learning. However, their differences can be considerable, and they can by no means be understood simply in terms of the word used to describe them. Each particular use of writing needs to be examined in its own context.

The areas of application are as diverse as the names, though they do give us a better insight into their uses. Writing is being applied in a whole host of areas, eg in counselling (Eldridge, 1983), psychology (Progoff, 1975; Hettich, 1976), sociology (Miller and Sieden Miller, 1976), management (Leary, 1981; Pedler, Burgoyne and Boydell, 1978), administration (Wolf, 1980), and epidemiology (Bawden and McKinnon, 1980). In the references given, we see examples of professional people exploring how journals and portfolios can be effectively used in their areas of competence. Some are asking how they can be used for student assessment (Houston, 1981; Romey, 1976; Bawden and McKinnon, 1980). Others are using them to come to a greater understanding and appreciation of their students through the unfolding of their autobiography (Butler, 1982; Stansbury, 1980; Powell in Chapter 2). A few have begun to reflect more explicitly on the relationship between writing and learning in general (Christenson, 1981; Yinger and Clark, 1981; Rainer, 1980).

Writing has always been used in human history to record events of all kinds, but we also find more personal uses of writing in which individuals recorded their insights into life. The most ancient document of this kind that I am familiar with is the *Meditations* of Marcus Aurelius from the second century (Penguin edition, 1964). It records the reflections of this Roman emperor, and provides an insight into his reminiscences about life. Other examples of this type of document are the *Pensées* of Pascal, from the seventeenth century (Penguin edition, 1961), and in this century the *Markings* of Dag Hammerskjold (1964). These documents are personal jottings of men who have reflected deeply on the meaning of life. However, they do not contain, nor were they meant to contain, any principles about the use of writing for others. In our own century, certain figures have arisen who have contributed significantly to conceptualizing principles about the use of writing. Rainer points to four main figures: Carl Jung, Marion Milner, Ira Progoff, and Anaïs Nin.

> Each of them, in an individual way, pointed out how the diary permits its writer to tap valuable inner resources. And they developed techniques that aid this process. Jung emphasized the importance of recording dreams and inner imagery; Milner, the usefulness of intuitive writing and drawing; Progoff popularized techniques for uncovering an inner destiny; and Anaïs Nin demonstrated the creative fulfilment achieved through listening for and valuing one's feelings. All of them recognized a need in the modern world to reflect calmly upon knowledge that comes from within. (Rainer, 1980, p21)

The many efforts to explore the use of writing mentioned above are an application of the principles that have emerged, and, in some cases, a further development of them. While significant figures open important doors, the way beyond them is often found by the many who patiently apply the newfound insight to the manifold areas of human experience. This chapter records one such application to the area of leadership.

To describe the method outlined within this chapter I have chosen the word 'portfolio'. Its meaning will unfold as it is described, and I consider it to be applicable to any method similar to what is described here. For me the word 'portfolio' means a work-book, a forum within which one works seriously with the experiences of learning or life. It fosters that important and essential counterpart to experience: reflection. However, it is not the word but the reality that is important, and it is the latter that is being described here.

I have used this method of writing within the context of a one-year full-time programme providing leadership development to people who would be exercising leadership within religious communities. Most of the participants were aged between 35 and 50, and were, for the most part, well motivated and anxious to participate fully in the programme. The portfolio was used to assist participants with the whole programme, rather than as an aid or assessment for any one unit within it. All members of staff encouraged the participants to use the portfolio within their respective courses.

The precise focus of the programme was to provide education for leadership within the area of religious development. The leadership role of the participants at the conclusion of the programme would be one of helping other members of their communities with their personal religious growth. The knowledge and skills necessary to achieve this were presented to them within the context of their own personal religious development. Therefore, within the programme, special attention was given to the growth of each participant as a person and as a believer. The programme was directed to helping participants come to an appreciation of personal and religious growth by assisting them to reflect on these realities in their own lives. The participants themselves were recognized as being one of the most important resources of the programme, and they were encouraged to interact with each other, and share the growth that had taken place, and was taking place within them. The aim of the portfolio was to aid reflection on their own personal development and to encourage them to share this with others. The following goals for the portfolio were presented to the participants.

1. To provide a record of the significant learning experiences that have taken place.
2. To help the participant come into touch and keep in touch with the self-development process that is taking place for them.
3. To provide the participants with an opportunity to express, in a personal and dynamic way, their self-development.
4. To foster a creative interaction
   -- between the participant and the self-development process that is taking place.
   -- between the participant and other participants who are also in the process of self-development.
   -- between the participant and the facilitator whose role it is to foster such self-development.
5. To provide a means of reflecting on one's commitment to, and involvement in, the leadership programme.

Keeping the Portfolio

At the beginning of each year, some introductory advice was given to the participants on how to approach the portfolio. Over the years this has grown. At the end of each year, I have asked the participants to write down suggestions that they would make to someone just beginning to use a portfolio. What follows is drawn from their responses and from my own experience. The views expressed will not always be in quotations, but frequently will reflect the language of our participants.

1. The portfolio is meant to be a very personal document: there is no right or wrong way to keep it. Seek out the method that suits you best. It is very important to keep the portfolio personal. It is to be shaped by your own talents and needs. Its usefulness can be in proportion to the extent to which it is your own. It is an extention of yourself, not something outside of you. In it you can and should

say what you feel. It is important to be yourself; that what you write is important to you, not just what other people say is important.

2. Be frank and honest in your entries. One participant put it this way: 'Write it as it is, not as you would like it to be, nor as you think it should be.' Be open and sincere in what you record.
3. Have a positive approach to the portfolio. Recognize the potential that it has, and approach it as something that can give rich return. Do not be afraid of the exercise. One participant put it well: 'Treat it as a close friend — not as an enemy or stranger.'
4. Be aggressive in approaching the portfolio. Do not dally round working out how you are going to do it; get down and do something. A number of participants advised 'write, write, write'; the more one plans, the less spontaneous it can be. Let it flow, uncensored, and in whatever order it comes. It is very useful simply to write, and then to reflect on what has been written.
5. Feel free to express yourself in diagrams, pictures, through cuttings or other types of material. Sometimes a symbol can express what we are trying to say better than we can.
6. The portfolio is meant to be a work-book. Entries are to be worked through a number of times, and important aspects of them highlighted. Therefore, underlining, circling, different coloured inks, and anything else that will draw out significant things should be used. As the year progresses, it is important to go back to the very early entries in the portfolio and to reflect further on them. It may be necessary to leave some space after each entry for recording later reflections.
7. Be spontaneous, use your own words, put your own names on things. Say what you feel, and if that makes you feel guilty, record that and work with it further. Do not be concerned about how you write. Do not look for style or literary eloquence, or worry that your writing does not seem to be great stuff.
8. Take up issues that surface when you are working with the portfolio. Do not let other things take your attention. Focus on the things that are important, and do not waste time in trivialities.
9. Do not be rigid in the way you keep the portfolio, but rather be prepared to change if necessary. Feel free to try different methods, so that you can mould this exercise to your personal talents and needs. 'It became easier and more meaningful once I discovered my own style of keeping the portfolio.'
10. Be faithful to it; persevere in the face of initial difficulties in keeping the portfolio. 'Stick at it,' was common advice given by past participants.
11. Record the experiences as soon as possible after they happen, and as fully as possible. Some participants found it helpful to carry a little notebook with them, so that they could jot down the feelings, behaviour, or thoughts that occurred throughout the day. There is a very definite advantage in being able to record things as quickly as possible, even though one may not immediately write them up fully.

12. Have a regular time also to write in the portfolio, and a fixed time each week to reflect back on it. To use it to fullest advantage, it is important to read over it frequently. It is not just writing in it that is important, but the continuing reflection on what has been written. One of the great enemies of the portfolio is procrastination. I have found that it is best to recommend to the students that they have fixed times and then try hard to stick to them, without necessarily making them absolutely exclusive.

13. Many participants suggest that important issues in the portfolio need to be shared with others. Talking about one's ideas, thoughts and reflections will bring feedback that can help deepen them. These deepenings should then be recorded in the portfolio.

14. Feel free to seek help with the portfolio from others; fellow participants, other people who have used this type of exercise, or the facilitators of the programme. Sharing among participants can be helpful. However, it is important that individual participants are not put off, or feel overshadowed, by what others are doing. It is important that the individual takes the help that is needed, without feeling that he or she has to conform to what other people are doing, and the way they are doing it. Openness to share with others and openness to listen to others are two important aspects in keeping the portfolio.

15. It is recommended that a loose-leaf folder be used for this exercise. This enables the insertion of new pages if previously reflected on experiences need more reflection. It also means that material can be rearranged within the portfolio. Some participants said that it is helpful to rearrange material under headings that bring similar material together. It is important to date each entry in the portfolio, so that rearrangement does not destroy the sequence of what has been written down.

16. Be selective. Most participants recognized that in the beginning they wrote a great deal more than was necessary. Selectivity was a sign of experience in using the portfolio.

Within our programme, one and a half hours each week for the first term were devoted to assisting the participants' work with the portfolio. Participants were encouraged and helped to share with each other what they were doing in the portfolio. This meant not just a sharing of the content, where that was appropriate, but also the method which each was using. I found this helpful, as participants learned from each other techniques that could help them, techniques which had not occurred to them personally. During these sessions, I would also provide exercises which would expose participants to techniques they could use. Rainer (1980) records some basic diary devices: writing for catharsis, making descriptions of events and free writing from intuition. She also singles out and explains seven special techniques: the use of a list, construction of portraits, sketching maps of consciousness, use of guided imagery, seeing things from an altered point of view, writing unsent letters and imaginary dialogues with others. I would offer an exercise in devices or techniques such as these, so that by doing them within the learning context, the participants would take them up more confidently in their own time.

An important instruction given to the students was that the portfolio would be absolutely confidential. This meant that participants would not be asked to hand in the portfolio, or, at any stage, to let it leave their own hands. This was done to try to ensure that the participants really did use the portfolio to work with the issues that were most personally important for them. They were told, however, that they would be asked to share from the portfolio. This meant that in group situations they would be called on to share with other participants some of the issues that they had included in their portfolio. It was stressed, however, that they would be fully in control of whatever was shared, and they would only share those things with which they were comfortable. In fact most of the students did hand their portfolio to the facilitator to seek some response on how they were working with it. Most would also have shared the portfolio with selected participants, close friends and advisors. Over the three years I have never been tempted to reverse the emphasis on confidentiality. I have found that it helps make the portfolio a more personal, and therefore a more creative and productive instrument.

Feedback from participants suggests that the portfolio would be less personal if it had to be handed in to be checked. Quite a number suggested that it would be a different document if it had to be evaluated by staff members. They said that, if it had to be handed in, it would become something written for someone else rather than for themselves. This would have taken away one of its most important characteristics. A minority suggested that, since they had given it to some staff members anyway, the obligation to hand it in would not have changed the way they kept it.

How Participants Used the Portfolio

Even though participants were left free to use the portfolio in their own way, common elements appeared in their use of it. Some suggestions had been made about what could be included in it: information from lectures, interpretations and applications of material, affective response to the learning experiences, personal behaviour and personal evaluation. However, these suggestions were general enough to let each person proceed in his or her own way. The following paragraphs offer some insight into how the participants used the portfolio, what they recorded in it, and how it helped them. Where the text appears in quotation marks I am recording the words of the participants, taken from their post-course evaluations of the use of the portfolio.

The portfolio was widely used to provide a permanent record of their personal journey, as a basis for continuing reflection. 'I have used the portfolio to record meaningful experiences, which then became more meaningful after the first articulation — and led to further reflection and articulation. It helped me to surface what was operating within me in situations in which I was deeply involved.' 'The keeping of a portfolio made it possible to knit the year's progress by reading back and considering what I had written in the light of the present and vice versa. It made possible a stepping back and having a wider perspective.'

It enabled the participants to keep track of what was happening in their development, and gave them ongoing access to it. It actually helped them appreciate life and learning as a journey. 'The portfolio has helped me learn about the learning process itself. It has opened to me the possibility and given me the encouragement to explore my own issues. The portfolio has become a silent teacher.' It enabled them to see areas of growth and lack of growth, and to observe growth actually taking place. Changes in attitudes, values and behaviour were apparent over the 12 months. In this context, the portfolio provided a useful means of monitoring growth and evaluating it at various stages, and, in a final way, at the end of the programme.

The portfolio provided for them an objectivity which helped participants deal more effectively and constructively with experiences in their lives. 'Yes, the keeping of the portfolio has facilitated my ability to share the experience which I recorded in it. It allows one to share objectively and fruitfully — once you've written something down — one views it more clearly. Once it's brought out into the open it loses its power and you are able to look at it and say "Well, there it is, this is part of me!" Effectively, it means "I'm owning it openly! It releases me psychologically".' The effort to describe issues from their personal lives helped them to clarify the dynamics that were actually taking place within them. This helped them to be able to consider the issues more objectively. The persons involved in the programme were often skilled in assisting other people to handle personal issues. However, when these same issues occurred in their own life, they were often too close to be able to recognize them and work with them. The portfolio provided them with an opportunity to clarify these issues and then, because they were openly expressed, bring to bear on them the skills that they have used in relation to others, but had not been able to use effectively in relation to themselves.

Nearly all mentioned that material from the formal educational exercises of the programme was included in the portfolio. Perhaps more accurately, it was responses to this material that were recorded. 'I used the portfolio to reflect further on the subject matter in relation to my own development.' 'The portfolio has helped me learn about the contents of the subjects. It has put them in the perspective of my personal history and experience and provided an umbrella under which significant insights can be linked together.' 'The portfolio helped me to learn about the content of the subjects: often subject areas have led me to a reflection on my understanding and acceptance of the content as it affects me here and now and in the future.' 'It helped me to correlate much of the lecture material; it was a link between the specifics of the programme and life away from it: it showed me the value of reflection on my experience, and the articulation of my reflections.'

It was the material which touched them personally which was most often recorded; that 'which has moved me in some way, for example, to look at myself, my attitudes and values, and to challenge them at times.' It did not matter whether the material came from the formal educational experiences, or other aspects of the programme, or from their personal life, it was what was meaningful to them that came to be recorded and considered. It was the personal appropriation of the material that was achieved through the portfolio. It was an instrument that helped serious thinking: 'any deep thinking that I needed to do, I found more beneficial if I wrote it into the portfolio.' This helped to raise their level of awareness, so that they came to be more observant in recognizing situations which might lead them to deeper insights.

As the programme was one of a religious nature, and directed towards leadership in spiritual development, many of the experiences and reflections recorded were related to religious issues. Personal attitudes to God, and experiences of prayer were often subjects for reflection. Within this context too, relationships with others were often worked through. Quite often, it was these religious reflections that provided a broad framework for a lot of the other work that was done within the programme.

For many participants, the portfolio opened up insights into their inner journey. 'This is a most fascinating feedback. I could go right to the core. Things became clear in my head as I wrote them down. It checks out why I do things. It helped me to put meaning to it.' They found that they were able to look at themselves within this confidential sphere with fewer inhibitions and more honesty. 'The portfolio helped me directly reflect on the most personally meaningful and important events of the year, by providing an objective avenue. It has to be honest otherwise I'm fooling myself and it is an utter waste of time. So if you're going to take it seriously then what goes down is important to me and the technique of describing the actual event without any interpretation ensures (at times brutal) honesty without pretence — a very necessary requisite if I really want to see what the real me is all about.' Even though when writing for oneself one can tend still not to be honest, they found it more difficult to be so within the framework of the portfolio. 'I wasn't afraid to be honest — well, I was afraid, but I tried to be honest just the same.' 'The portfolio did contribute significantly to my experience of the year. I found it an enriching experience overall. I found it a very liberating experience to be able to express what I was feeling as I was feeling it — to be utterly frank and open. But I also thought it was a scary experience as I pushed away the overcoat of defences that had kept a lot of strong feelings or hard thoughts at bay. Working through this was hard, damned hard, at times.'

They found that they were facing questions which formerly they were unable to face. It was not easy to ignore or shelve the issues when one actually had to write about them. One participant was led to face up to her refusal to consider herself a leader because she described in the portfolio something that took place during one of the lectures:

> I read the word 'leadership' on the screen (the other heading I skimmed over). He was working with a chart. I wanted to physically back away. I sat there registering waves of fright. I felt I did not want the word 'leader' applied to me. I remembered that I very rarely told anyone that I was to do a Leadership Programme, I simply described the course.

This facing up to uncomfortable issues in an honest way was one of the most fruitful effects of the portfolio for many. 'It has enabled me to reflect without inhibitions on my inward journey and so has opened me to questions I have formerly been afraid to know.' It meant that the real issues being raised by the programme were being faced. The nature of the programme in which these participants were involved was one that was directed towards self-development, rather than information about certain subjects. There was information provided that was important for them to learn, but the learning was always seen in terms of a personal integration of that material with a view to growth and later application.

Some used the portfolio to help them articulate their thoughts and feelings more concretely, and especially in their own words. This ability to put in their own words their deep feelings was particularly important for many. 'Yes, writing down my experiences, I became more conscious of what I am really feeling, and doing and "being" — I have found words to describe myself and so it is much easier to speak about myself to others.' It enabled them to identify and own these feelings and to appreciate them the more once they had named them in a way that was personally meaningful to them. 'Writing down what had happened or how I had been affected by happenings helped to identify feelings, keep things in perspective and often indicated the direction of my thoughts. My motivation often became clear as I wrote.' 'Helped me remember and recall later many aspects of various experiences that I otherwise would have forgotten. Many smaller issues would not have been "looked at" as fully and a characteristic pattern of feelings/behaviour in certain ways would be less likely to have been identified or if already recognized, nothing more effective in terms of change would have been done about what needed to be changed.'

For many the self-expression involved in keeping the portfolio brought with it self-knowledge, so that the portfolio was an important instrument of self-knowledge for them. 'Yes, the portfolio has helped me learn about myself, especially in retrospect when I read over a recalled experience. It's like a mirror that reflects me to myself.' 'The portfolio has helped me learn about myself. The questions raised have usually caused me to reflect very much on my own inner thoughts, feelings, and false ideas of myself built up over the years. Every part of the portfolio shows me in a very personal way.' For some, it fulfilled a desire to write. They found in it a means of creative self-expression. This ability to express themselves, and to embody their thoughts and feelings in their own words, meant that there were many feelings and insights captured that might otherwise have been lost. Not only were they captured, but they were embodied in a way that enabled the participant to work more constructively and effectively with them. The portfolio was like a friend in whom they could confide, and who could draw out of them things that otherwise would have remained unsaid, or perhaps would not even have been felt. They shared with it their insights, questions, fears, hopes and a wide variety of feelings. It was totally receptive and enabled them to express themselves freely. One participant said of it: 'it took a "pen-bashing" that I couldn't subject anyone else to. It didn't stare, yawn or get up and walk away.'

Advantages and Disadvantages

As the director of the programme, I found important advantages in fostering the use of the portfolio. It did meet the aims that were set down. Student feedback over three years suggested that they were met to a high degree. The most important aim was the facilitating of an interaction between students and the personal growth taking place within them. There was also creative action among those who worked well with the portfolio. The ability to express what was taking place in the participant meant that each was able to share it in his or her own words with the other participants and with the facilitators. Participants could communicate better because they had found a language in writing down their experiences in their own words. This meant that they could speak about the issues more easily in a group situation. They were also helped by the fact that their personal concerns were given an objectivity which, to a certain extent, separated them from themselves. This meant that they were able to talk about them more easily. I have found that there is sometimes personal material which participants want to share but are not able to because of an inability to express or communicate it. The portfolio enables such material to be shared. In a programme like ours, where the participants are a major resource, such facility in communication and the fostering of it are of great importance. I have found the portfolio to be very helpful in this regard.

Some participants considered that the time taken by the use of the portfolio was a disadvantage. One student described this lack of time in the following way: 'It takes a great deal of time, and I never had enough time to record all I wanted to. There was so much material surfacing for me that I had to end up being selective about what I wrote, thus leaving out some things I wish I had included.' This participant points to the need for selectivity. One of the most important things that the participant has to learn in using this exercise is to be selective. It is better to select a few things to record, and work with them at greater depth, rather than record many things. I felt the inclination of the participants initially was to record as much as possible, and the recognition that they had to record less, and work with it more, was a very important development within them. While the time it took did appear to be a disadvantage on the part of the participant, in the eyes of the facilitator the time devoted to the portfolio was often worthwhile and considered to be more important than the participants had judged it to be. From the point of view of the facilitator, the portfolio certainly demands time, and this can be a disadvantage. While there was no obligation for participants to hand in their portfolio, most did so and asked for assistance with it. This would have occurred on more than one occasion. This meant that portfolios had to be read and given careful consideration, so that a thoughtful response could be given which would help the participants in its use. However, even if this is a disadvantage, I found it was worth whatever effort it demanded.

Another criticism of the portfolio highlighted the fact that it is not a technique that will appeal universally, or be used by every participant. Some saw it as a job to be done, so that it lost the aspect of creativity that was an important part of it. For those who were not able to handle it, the portfolio became a chore which dragged more and more as the year went on. I found it necessary at times to suggest that individual participants discontinue its use. It makes a great call on the personal discipline of the participant. While this is an important part of any participant's involvement in the programme, the portfolio or the use of writing often makes demands that many are not accustomed to meet. It is a disadvantage from the point of view of the facilitator that the portfolio cannot be used universally. Perhaps it is hardly fair to call this a disadvantage. Perhaps we should rather say that the facilitator needs to learn that there are people who, even with special help, will not use the portfolio effectively. It would be better in these circumstances to try to provide some other way for these students to achieve the goals that are set down for the portfolio. I would suggest that one be slow in discouraging its use. I have found that, with special help, most were able to cope with it. However, that special help required time which was one of the disadvantages for the facilitator.

The 'special help' mentioned above was usually more time spent with individual participants who were having difficulties with the portfolio. It often meant designing some exercise which would help them work through the difficulty they were having. There were several types of participant who found significant difficulties in keeping the portfolio, but over the three years they were a very small minority. Some tended to become too introspective, and needed help to adjust their focus. Some focused excessively on negative aspects of their life and work, and needed to be guided to look for more positive elements. Those who were frightened of the issues that the portfolio could raise needed special help. One participant described her situation in these words: 'I found it difficult to keep the portfolio because I was torn in conflict and wanted very much to avoid the issues which it raised. It was much easier to direct my attention to intellectual areas which were safe, not as problematic. It was

very difficult to face the emotional issues. Many of them I avoided recording because I told myself I had no right to feel the way I did.'
A supportive relationship with the facilitator can help this person become more comfortable with the issues that are being raised. However, this again requires giving individual attention to the student, and can take a lot of time.

An Aid to Reflection

The focus of this chapter is the relationship between writing and the process of reflection. It has emerged from what has been said that many of our participants were helped to a deeper reflection through the keeping of the portfolio. I would like now to draw out more explicitly some of the important aspects of the relationship between the use of writing and reflection.

An important contribution of writing is that it provides an objectivity in relation to the initial learning experience. It can clarify the initial experience by removing it from the clouds of subjective feeling that can obscure it. It is a way of distancing oneself from the experience, which has the effect of clarifying it and fostering the ability to work with it, so that the learner can draw out potential learning. It can focus the learner's attention on what actually happened in the initial learning experience. It helps distinguish between what happened and how the learner interpreted what happened, or experienced what actually happened. One participant commented: 'the portfolio has helped me learn about myself by reflecting on the actual event and not on my interpretation of it.' While it is useful to reflect on one's interpretation of an event, the recognition that the actual event was different from the way the learner interpreted it will help the learner understand more of the learning process itself. The initial learning experience is composed of the actual things that took place and how they were experienced by the learner. The more clearly those elements are recognized, the more fruitful will be the reflection that takes place on them.

The use of writing also captures the initial event in a way that enables it to be the basis of continuing and more developed reflection. Very often, when an event is reflected upon, the original event becomes shaped or coloured by that later reflection, so that it becomes obscure and is sometimes lost. It is interesting to have shared an experience with certain people and to hear them talk about that experience over the years. Sometimes you recognize that, as they have applied it to different situations in which they want to use it as an illustration, they have changed what actually took place in the initial event. By writing a description of the initial experience, it can be returned to without being lost. The experience is also preserved in such a way that the learner can return to it when further knowledge has been gained which might help to interpret it more fully.

I have found that the use of writing in the learning situation helps learners recognize and take account of affective aspects of the learning process. It not only helps them appreciate the role of feeling, and clarify the feelings involved, it also helps them name these feelings and own them by expressing them in their own words. I have found our participants to be much more aware of the importance of feelings in learning, and they have come to be much more observant of the feelings that are actually present in a given situation than they were at the beginning of our programme. The awareness of feeling in the initial learning situation can lead to important learning. Why this or that particular affective response occurred in the initial learning experience can help learners appreciate the way they experience events. The way the learning exercise was experienced can give an insight into the way the learner experiences the world in general. Therefore whatever feelings are observed can be the basis of reflection that can lead to a deeper appreciation of the learning process and of the learner's way of experiencing.

However, sometimes the feelings that emerge in the initial learning experience actually obstruct further working with it. Until these feelings have been handled, the learner is not able to go on and be involved in reflection. Sometimes the recognition of obstructing emotions is sufficient to enable the learner to deal with them. They can be taken into account as the reflection process begins, and the person is in control enough not to let them distort or obstruct learning, even though they would have done this if the learner had not acknowledged their presence. There are other types of obstructing emotions, however, which may need to be discharged before enlightened reflection can take place. I have found that sometimes the learner can discharge these feelings by writing about them in the portfolio. Often, through a form of intensive writing, in which participants simply get out on to paper what they are feeling, there is sufficient discharge to free the learner to begin to reflect. However, on other occasions, the obstructing feelings may need to be worked with in a more formal way. In this case, it is not just a question of intensive writing about the feelings, but it may involve focusing on this issue, rather than on the material or subject matter that was intended in the initial learning experience.

Another significant element in reflection is the association of ideas: the bringing together of new and old in a way that can be the basis of working to integrate them. The material that our participants worked with in their portfolio was often what touched them in a particular way during the more formal educational exercises. What was said actually touched a chord within, and a relationship was born. This coming together of something new and something old was often a momentary thing that needed to be allowed to develop and grow. Towards the end of some lectures, I would ask the participants to do an exercise in writing. Through the use of intensive writing, ie encouraging the student simply to write without spending time in preparation, or in organizing thoughts, I found that material that had touched a person was able to be expressed in a way that, as it were, unlocked a whole area for the participant. The writing about the particular incident, the specific experience of being touched by new knowledge, seemed to bring with it a whole association of feelings and ideas that were within the participant. It was like opening a door and having the contents of a room fall out. This then had to be worked with, and it was. However, through the use of writing, the material that was to be processed surfaced and was captured.

It was often at this time that the participants found it necessary to face what had been revealed. Sometimes what emerged was such that it took great courage for the participant to go on. The difficulty often lay not in working with it, but rather acknowledging it, appropriating it, owning it, being willing to accept that this was the 'real me'. This stage often exposed the false images that we have of ourselves. Only when such falseness was acknowledged could the participant really enter into the work of reflection.

The portfolio helped participants to integrate existing and new knowledge. The use of writing can create in the person a dynamic in which the person's existing knowledge is held in a more fluid state so that whatever new knowledge comes, it can be more easily integrated within it. The creative interaction between the person and the person's self-development helps incorporate new realities into that self-development. It can prevent the situation arising where new knowledge lies on top of old knowledge, without integration taking place. Creative interaction with one's own development helps to ensure that new knowledge is incorporated in, and integrated with, existing knowledge.

Our participants found that by noting important learning experiences, and by recording their reflection on them, they were much more aware of the growth taking place. They could actually see the learning process as it was unfolding in their life. This meant that they were not just taking new knowledge, and integrating it into their life, but they were also learning about the process by which that was being done. The use of writing was not only helping them to reflect and learn, but also helping them to appreciate the actual process of reflection within learning.

Introducing the Portfolio

As this chapter is meant to help readers introduce writing as an aid to reflection into their own learning or teaching method, I will conclude with some further practical suggestions, arising from my own experience, which might help facilitate its introduction in other situations.

1. Initiate the student into the use of the portfolio by definite exercises in writing. The student needs to be encouraged to write, write, write and from this experience of writing, the principles of the portfolio should be drawn out. I have found the devices and techniques presented by Rainer (1980) helpful in this regard. The writing itself creates the dynamics that are operative in the use of the portfolio, or any type of journal. The key to success in using the journal is to encourage the students to write.

2. Suggest to the students that they have a definite time each day or week in which they work with the portfolio, and a definite duration of time. Students will not work with the portfolio successfully if they only pick it up when they feel like it.

3. It is not enough simply to do a lot of work at the beginning of a programme and then leave the students to work with the portfolio throughout it. I have found that periodically one needs to review how the portfolio is going and to provide more exercises that will assist the students with it. In fact, the exercises should be graded so that later exercises to which these students are exposed should be more demanding than those which are presented initially.

4. It is extremely helpful to the person keeping the portfolio if there exists a good relationship with the facilitator; one that will allow the student to share the portfolio with the facilitator. This personal response to what the student is doing is a major help in working with the portfolio. However, it requires a good rapport with the facilitator, because of the personal nature of what has been written.

5. I would encourage those who wish to use the portfolio with their students to begin, and not wait until they have a completely well-developed system to use. Even though the facilitator may not be adept in the use of writing as an aid to reflection, there is much that the students can gain as they work with it and help the facilitator to come to greater experience in its use. It is better to get in and give it a go, than spend a lot of time finding out about it and waiting until you have found out all about it before starting.

6. I would encourage facilitators to mould the use of writing to their own talents and needs. It is not necessary just to take up somebody else's model and use it in your situation. Look to the principles that are involved in writing, and endeavour to put together something that will be a natural part of your approach and an integral part of your programme.

7. Constantly encourage students to continue to work with experiences that have been recorded in the past. I have found that students often need a nudge to keep working with a particular experience. There is a tendency to think that, once it has been reflected upon, it is worked through. I have found it necessary to point out that the incident or experience can be worked through again when the participant's powers of reflection have been deepened. A definite time at regular intervals needs to be devoted to going back over past incidents.

8. I have found it helpful also to recommend to students that they take time at definite intervals to read the portfolio as a whole. Not just work with particular exercises but actually sit down and read the work as a whole. This gives them something of an idea of the development that has taken place and very often will help them to relate different incidents and reflections that have been recorded.

9. Encourage students to record less and reflect more. There is a tendency at the beginning to write down many things. This cuts back the time

that is available for reflection on them. The more the student is able to be aware that it is the depth of reflection on the experience rather than the number of experiences that is important, the better it will be. The student has to learn to be selective.

10. I would recommend that the portfolio be kept as a personal document. There is a lot to be gained from having access to a student's portfolio, but the consequences of this access are very often that the student writes the portfolio for the teacher, and the more fundamental dynamics that are taking place are not recorded. It has been my practice to let the portfolio be primarily a work for the participant, and therefore its focus is on how the participant uses it and learns about himself or herself, rather than seeing it as a means whereby the facilitator can gain insight into the life and processes of the student, even though very often it can fulfil this latter role.

11. Fostering interaction among participants using the portfolio can be very helpful. I would suggest that this type of interaction be focused in two areas: first, on the method that they are using in the portfolio and how it is helping them. This would help others to appreciate what can be achieved through the portfolio, and might give them some ideas on how to use it. Second, to gain further reflection and feedback on the experiences of the portfolio and the reflections that have been made on them. This means sharing the content of the portfolio, and could only be done with matter that participants are comfortable with. However, its advantages are that it brings another mind, with a different way of seeing things, to bear on the particular experience and on the reflections that have taken place on it. Very often another person will contribute new thoughts, observe new elements, and stimulate the student to reflections that would hitherto have been unavailable. Students working together can motivate each other and help sustain interest in the exercise. It is possible to work seriously in a group on the use of writing without necessarily jeopardizing the confidentiality that has been recommended.

12. While the confidentiality of the portfolio should be kept, and students should not be placed in situations where they are forced to violate it, it is good to provide for participants an opportunity to share it in an environment which leaves them free to control completely the method of sharing. I have found that, even though there are many things in the portfolio that would not be revealed, after working with some very serious things, students do feel able to talk about them in an appropriate forum.

13. I would recommend that the focus of the portfolio, or the use of writing, be the integration of new knowledge into the personal development of the participant. This focus brings together many of the important aspects of learning, and will develop the potential of the portfolio to the fullest extent.

14. It is good to introduce an element of fun into the keeping of the portfolio: a sharing of amusing insights that have emerged, or the use

of cartoons to sum up a situation. Some lighthearted activity can successfully impart the important principles and foster interest in the portfolio. I think the use of the portfolio is marred by an excessive seriousness. I have found that people who take it too seriously are often the ones who become too introspective in its use.

I have found the portfolio a very helpful learning tool. It has become an important part of my approach to teaching and in designing new programmes. I always include within them a portfolio element. One of the great pleasures of my work is to see students take up this instrument of learning, make it their own, and launch themselves on a journey of self-discovery. I hope that, through the inclusion of the portfolio in your teaching method, you will experience the same joy.

References

Bawden, R and McKinnon, C (1980) The portfolio, *HERDSA News*, **2**, 2, pp4-5

Butler, S (1982) Assessing the journal: an exercise in self-evaluation, *English Quarterly*, 14, 4, pp75-83

Christensen, R S (1981) 'Dear diary': a learning tool for adults, *Lifelong Learning: the Adult Years*, **5**, 2, pp4-5 and 31

Eldridge, W D (1983) The use of personal logs to assist clinical students in understanding and integrating theories of counselling intervention, *Instructional Science*, 12, pp279-283

Hammerskjold, D (1964) *Markings*, London: Faber and Faber

Hettich, P (1976) The journal: an autobiographical approach to learning, *Teaching of Psychology*, 3, pp60-63

Houston, G (1981) How am I going to award myself a diploma? *Educational Change and Development*, 3, 2, pp37-46

Leary, M (1981) Working with biography, in Boydell, T and Pedler, M (eds) *Management Self-Development: Concepts and Practices*, Aldershot: Gower

Marcus Aurelius (1964) *Meditations*, Harmondsworth: Penguin Books

Miller, R and Seiden Miller, R (1976) The student's sociological diary, *Teaching Sociology*, 4, 1, pp67-82

Pascal, B (1961) *The Pensées*, Harmondsworth: Penguin Books

Pedler, M, Burgoyne, J and Boydell, T (1978) *A Manager's Guide to Self-Development*, London: McGraw-Hill

Progoff, I (1975) *At a Journal Workshop: The Basic Text and Guide for Using the Intensive Journal*, New York: Dialogue House Library

Rainer, T (1980) *The New Diary*, London: Angus and Robertson

Romey, B (1976) *Confluent Education in Science*, Canton: Ash Lad Press

Stansbury, D (1980) The record of personal experience, in Burgess, T and Adams, E (eds) *Outcomes of Education*, London: MacMillan

Wolf, J F (1980) Experiential learning in professional education: concept and tools, *New Directions in Experiential Learning*, **8**, pp17-26

Yinger, R J and Clark, C M (1981) *Reflective Journal Writing: Theory and Practice* East Lansing: Michigan State University, The Institute for Research on Teaching

CHAPTER 4
Debriefing in Experience-based Learning

Margot Pearson, *New South Wales Department of Technical and Further Education*
David Smith, *University of Sydney*

Every day each one of us is involved in a multitude of experiences. Some experiences are based on habit, some the product of social mores and societal expectations, still others are new, different and challenging. Through each experience we may gain new understandings and skills, and our beliefs about ourselves, others and the world are challenged, changed or reinforced. The old adage of 'experience is the best teacher' still holds true to some extent.

Simply to experience, however, is not enough. Often we are so deeply involved in the experience itself that we are unable, or do not have the opportunity, to step back from it and reflect upon what we are doing in any critical way. In any planned activity for learning, debriefing provides an opportunity to engage in this reflection, whether the activity is part of on-the-job training, in-service education, work-experience programmes, on-site project work, or staff training and development exercises (eg in-basket activities, role-playing exercises, operating simulators, or simulation games).

In this chapter we will outline the central importance of debriefing in experience-based learning, discuss some of the important issues connected with debriefing as a means of promoting reflection, and suggest a variety of ways to develop more effective debriefing in a variety of experience-based learning situations. In particular we will consider the nature of debriefing and its relationship to briefing, its purposes and the relationship of these to different types of knowledge being processed, and various ways to organize debriefing. We conclude with some suggestions that, if employed, can render the debriefing experience more effective.

The Nature of Debriefing

The historical roots of debriefing lie in military campaigns and war games. Debriefing was the time after a mission or exercise when participants were brought together to describe what had occurred, to account for the actions that had taken place, and to develop new strategies as a result of the experience. This function of debriefing in relation to military action and training still continues today and in a number of ways the original purposes of debriefing are directly relevant to programmes of experience-based learning. However, debriefing in regard to experiences in these programmes is more than simply describing events or accounting for actions. Debriefing provides the opportunity for structured reflection whereby experiences are used for experience-based learning.

Debriefing is sometimes identified with other terms such as 'publishing' and 'generalizing', which are used in experiential learning models. These terms refer to steps in the debriefing process. Similarly the whole process of debriefing is sometimes referred to as 'processing'. Whatever the terms used, debriefing is that phase in experience-based learning where purposeful reflection by an individual or group takes place.

This debriefing can occur either immediately after an experience or sometimes later. It can have many purposes and dimensions, as will be discussed; however, debriefing is not therapy, counselling or encountering, although sometimes elements of these types of activities are present, especially in small group settings (Harvey, 1979). Neither is debriefing simply 'having a chat', or 'rapping' about what happened in the experience. Experiences in learning programmes are underlaid by intentions. Although it may be possible to consider debriefing as something occurring after a spontaneous experience, generally it is associated with purposeful and planned activity, usually within a total learning programme. It is debriefing in this context that is discussed in this chapter.

Active experience is involving and interesting, even exciting. Debriefing means the cessation of this experiencing and the deliberate decision to reflect then on action. Often it is difficult to stop an activity and encourage participants to begin the debriefing phase of a learning experience. To accomplish debriefing successfully, there must be a strong commitment by a group leader to its importance and this commitment must also be transferred to the participants, which is not always an easy task.

Effective debriefing also requires time. This time has to be included in the planning of any experience-based programme. Too often it is the debriefing phase of a programme which is cancelled or considerably shortened by the extension of the activity itself. Thus the commitment to the importance of debriefing must be accompanied by a commitment by the group leader to allow sufficient time for effective debriefing to occur. As a general rule, the length of time for debriefing should not be less than the time taken for the activity itself. One of the writers, working with student teachers, finds that 40 minutes, the usual time period of a normal lesson in secondary schools, is the minimum time required to debrief an observed lesson with a student teacher. In most cases to complete debriefing effectively takes more time than the activity itself. This is especially so with a group experience where often all participants will need to be involved which necessitates more time.

Debriefing can be structured to occur in only one session, or it may occur a number of times during a programme. If the programme is an extended one, debriefing sessions may be needed at the end of any particular activity before going on to the next, as well as occurring at the conclusion of the programme as a whole.

It is possible to draw a distinction between what might be called 'formal debriefing' and 'informal debriefing'. Formal debriefing is that which occurs in the presence of a group leader and is deliberately structured in some manner. Informal debriefing is that which occurs individually or with others after formal debriefing. What should be remembered is that the products of informal debriefing may be just as important and powerful as those of formal debriefing. Which is more important of these two types of debriefing is a question for much greater research. In the literature of simulation gaming, for example, the place of formal debriefing is strongly defended. However, its relationship to informal debriefing is still highly problematic. Certainly one of the aims of formal debriefing should be to stimulate participants so that they will continue reflecting upon the experience after the formal debriefing period has ended. The power to stimulate this continuing reflection by participants is related on the one hand to the careful planning and structuring of the formal debriefing period, and on the other to the managing of the debriefing process so that it does not finish in such a way as to inhibit further reflection by appearing to answer all questions and to close all doors.

Briefing and Debriefing

Formal debriefing is likely to be more effective when the purposes of a learning activity are clearly identified during a briefing phase preceding any activity. These purposes form a focus for the debriefing so that the beginning and the concluding phases of the learning activity provide an integrated context for the experience itself.

Briefing, like debriefing, derives its roots from military experience. It is the time when participants are oriented to the experience. They are provided with their instructions, goals and the rules within which they can achieve the goals. In some cases the rules relate to acceptable behaviour within a specific context; in others the rules set limits to actions or give set procedures (see Smith, 1981, for further details about briefing). For example, students preparing to enter work experience, training or practical programmes may be instructed in the expectation of dress and role relationships in their experiential learning settings. Rules may also concern the details of projects to be pursued. At other times rules may represent restrictions on participants' behaviour which are essential for the experience to unfold as intended. For example in a well-known game where groups must assemble pieces of paper into a square, no one is allowed to talk to the other participants (Mulford, 1977).

More important than the instructions and rules provided during the briefing stage are the purposes and intentions of the planners and leaders of the activities. Although debriefing may well include the discussion of issues that were not anticipated, the debriefing phase should attempt to achieve the purposes and intentions identified by the planners or leaders during the briefing and to evaluate how successfully this has been accomplished. The closeness of the relationship between briefing and debriefing will vary according to the outcomes being sought and the amount of control over the process by the leader.

Briefing, however, is not to be confused with 'giving the game away'. Clarifying intentions and giving procedures does not need to include giving the conclusions to be derived from the experience where these outcomes are to be discovered during the experience. If what is to be learned is given at the beginning of an activity, it will simply become a demonstration. For example, in a game about one-way communication, the group leader would establish the participants' roles, give them their instructions about what to do and establish that the game was intended to clarify our understanding of the communication process. The group leader would not pre-empt the debriefing by mentioning one-way communication or indicating that the game would show ineffective communication structures.

Stages in the Debriefing Process

There have been a number of steps or stages suggested for the debriefing process (eg Pfeiffer and Jones, 1975; van Ments, 1983). The stages can be summarized as a series of questions:

☐ What happened?
☐ How did the participants feel?
☐ What does it mean?

What Happened?
Debriefing should begin with non-threatening issues. Initially participants should be asked to describe what happened, their own and others' actions during the experience. This description provides a common starting point for everyone involved in the experience especially, as is often the case, when participants have undergone their experiences in different sites or in small groups. Such a beginning allows all participants basic knowledge concerning everyone else's experience. It facilitates comparisons with another's experience and suggests that one person's experience and reaction may be shared by other group members. Beginning in this way may well provide the group leader with issues, problems, reactions and feelings that need to be discussed further later in the debriefing session.

How Did the Participants Feel?
In this stage the group leader needs to ask all participants, usually starting with the main protagonists in a role-play or game, how they felt during the experience. Personal and interpersonal feelings and reactions are often explored and this may be threatening to some participants. However, this

stage is essential in the debriefing of any planned activity in an experience-based learning programme. Unfortunately, it is the stage of debriefing that is sometimes omitted or dealt with in a superficial manner. Jones (1968) criticized the use of the MACOS: Man A Course of Study programme in which he asserted that experiences and materials involving feelings about death and conflict were dealt with only at the intellectual level. If such feelings are not dealt with, the sharing of meaning and understandings can be blocked.

To deal with these feelings successfully an atmosphere of trust, acceptance of others and a willingness to take risks must be established. Accomplishing such an atmosphere is not easy. It requires the development of group-processing skills (Johnson, 1972; Watson, Vallee and Mulford, 1981)\and a sensitivity to the underlying feelings and emotions within the group. A group leader may also need skills in handling interpersonal anger and conflict and its resolution. Although anger and conflict are not necessarily triggered by every planned activity, often the reactions of individuals to other people with whom they are involved can lead to stored emotion and the need to release this. Even a seemingly innocuous activity may result in the expression of anger and conflict during the debriefing process. One writer can well remember the violent outburst of anger, envy and frustration by a student teacher as the result of hearing other students' accounts of practice teaching experiences in school sites which she saw as so much more positive than her own! Thus the group leader must always be prepared for a debriefing session that can quickly be characterized by unexpected expressions of emotion.

What Does it Mean?
A third stage in debriefing involves the participants in generalizing from the experience and their reactions to it. This can be a very exciting stage as participants grasp insights or several agree on a point that has been thoroughly thrashed out. The conclusions may not be unique or original but, in the process, individuals and the group achieve meaning that is personal and immediately relevant.

In the experience of the two writers, the sequential stage models suggested in the literature may be logical in theory but are not always practical. Often the debriefing process is directed by the most important issues of the participants. Sometimes these issues at the start of debriefing may be far more emotional than dealing with a description of the experience itself. The need for sequence and organization is probably directly related to the personality of the debriefer, his or her experience, and the needs of the participants. It is also related to the type of knowledge being processed and how this knowledge is acquired.

Debriefing, Knowledge and Ways of Knowing

Underlying the preceding discussion have been two dimensions that could be characterized as moving from low threat to high threat and from the concrete to the general. A further dimension relates to the types of knowledge outcomes of a learning activity and different ways of knowing this knowledge.

Knowledge, broadly defined, can be classified in a number of different ways (eg Phenix, 1964; Schwab, 1964; Hirst, 1974). For the purposes of this chapter we are going to classify it on the basis of how we know and come to understand different types of knowledge. If there are different ways in which human beings know, learn and understand, then this has important implications for the purposes of debriefing and the manner in which it is organized.

It has been suggested that there are at least three ways in which we come to know and understand things about the world (Habermas, 1971, 1974). Habermas was interested in different ways of validating knowledge: different methods of how people know that they know something. Habermas claimed that one way we know something is by empirical observation, especially observation of some phenomena a number of times. There are certain relationships between phenomena in the world that will occur in the same way time after time. For example, regardless of whether we understand the physical principle of the specific density of water, if we place a tray of water into the freezer of a working refrigerator, it will form ice.

Similarly there is what might be called conventional knowledge; that is knowledge which has been adopted, and is accepted by a particular culture. For example, although we cannot observe that two apples and two oranges together add up to four pieces of fruit, we know by conventional mathematics knowledge that they do. In the same way we cannot bid a French-speaking person 'good night' by saying *bonjour*. There is a great deal of knowledge then that is not problematic. It is knowledge which is accepted and about which there is little debate.

Another very important way we know is through sharing our meanings and our understanding through language. Thus if we want to know how a person felt in a particular situation, although we may have the opportunity to observe his or her behaviour and non-verbal actions, we must still interpret this and place our own meaning upon it. If we want to know if our meanings are correct, if we want to know how the person felt and experienced the situation, we must share our interpretations and negotiate with one another, using language to clarify and understand each other's meanings. Likewise if we wish to arrive at some common understanding of a concept such as 'democracy' we must share our interpretations and meanings using language.

A final way of knowing concerns knowing about ourselves, our theories and our actions within a context of the wider world. This 'critical' knowing also depends upon arriving at common meanings through language. However, it is more than simply interpretative understanding. Critical knowing is concerned with a critical understanding of the self, the manner in which we act, and the personal theories that inform our actions. Critical knowing results in a greater awareness and may provide the possibility to change our actions in the direction of more desired objectives. So, for example, if one of the aims of a training programme is to assist participants to become more aware of their own actions in decision-making and problem-solving, then the notion of critical knowing is central to that aim. The result of critical knowing is a more conscious awareness of why certain actions have taken place, the ideological or theoretical basis of the actions and whether there are more appropriate or effective action strategies that might be used (Kemmis et al, 1983). For example, in a role-play about reacting to a recently bereaved person, the person acting as a friend may have been soothing and used statements such as 'You'll be all right'. In debriefing the group leader might find that a group accepted this as appropriate behaviour and might consider confronting the participants with a statement such as 'But will she be all right?' or even in a trusting climate, 'Why do you want her to stop crying?' Such a question would challenge assumptions that the helper was primarily concerned to help the bereaved, and open up the opportunity to discuss the possibility that the helper is more concerned with protecting herself from the discomfort of overt expression of grief.

Although of necessity this account has been brief, it suggests there are different ways that we come to know, learn and understand. What is much more important, however, are the implications of each of these ways of knowing. Different types of knowledge suggest different forms and approaches to the debriefing process, and different relationships between participants and the group leader.

If the activity has been established to teach participants a particular set of procedures, conventions or practices that are part of a particular culture (eg teaching trade students the characteristics of certain materials, or a sequence of skills involved in a particular operation; teaching clerks or managers formats of documents that are used in a particular organization; teaching catering students the acceptable conventions of serving food and wine) the knowledge with which we are dealing is conventional, accepted and largely unproblematic. It does not basically rely on meaning but on selecting the appropriate components, procedures or behaviours.

Part of our debriefing, after experiences such as these, may very well be to establish to what degree participants have learnt and applied appropriately these practices and conventions. Since establishing whether this learning has taken place does not necessarily rely upon interpretative understanding, procedures involving pencil and paper formats may be very appropriate. Checklists, questionnaires, tests, written accounts of what people did may be very useful, along with aids such as photographs, films and videotapes of participants in action. For example, in the Royal Air Force, microcomputer gaming and closed-circuit television are used in an approach based on micro-teaching principles to train air-traffic control simulator instructors (McCarthy and Easby, 1983).

In dealing with conventional knowledge the group leader responsible for the debriefing may well remain in a position of power and authority as the holder of expert knowledge. Discussion is primarily to allow participants to clarify conventions and to allow the group leader to ensure that participants have integrated this knowledge into their experience. So there may be little need to have a great amount of interaction and discussion among participants.

Activities aimed at developing understanding and interpretation in contrast should involve high degrees of interpersonal action and relationships, and often the confrontation of deeply held personal and cultural beliefs and practices. Examples of such experiences are learning about client or colleague relationships, understanding different viewpoints and developing empathy with other people's circumstances. In all these cases debriefing, which centres upon the sharing of participants' reactions, meanings and understandings, is necessary to achieve the development of interpretative meaning and understanding.

The role of the group leader in this case is not one of an expert with power and authority but that of a leader facilitating a sharing of ideas and understandings. Formal pencil and paper instruments such as questionnaires and checklists may well be utilized. However, they cannot be the sole means of processing the experiences. If used, they are a means of focusing the individual's or group's thoughts upon the experiences. They are a means of eliciting more detailed information, understandings, emotions and actions to form the basis for further discussion.

Where the role of the debriefer is mainly to facilitate the sharing of the meanings and understandings of the participants, the debriefing session must be organized and structured in such a way as to promote feelings of comfort, safety, trust, risk and acceptance. An environment characterized by these features is essential for participants to feel that they can share their experiences in a frank, open and honest manner. In this context the group leaders will undertake a great deal of listening and encourage participants to talk with one another. The framework for the discussion will still be clearly related to the originally established intentions, but the leader will also be open to hearing the concerns of the participants and directing discussion towards these concerns. By example the group leader establishes and strengthens an accepting climate conducive to sharing. The leader in any initial discussion needs to be non-judgemental and refrain from re-interpreting participants' contributions by paraphrasing or summarizing.

Once a supportive climate has been established, this role of facilitating the sharing of participants' meanings and understandings and clarifying the feelings being expressed can involve a further development: that of challenging viewpoints expressed and the perceptions and theories on which they are based. Such confrontation is appropriate where the intention is to promote critical knowing. The major aim of debriefing sessions aimed towards critical knowing is to shift individuals' understanding of themselves and their own actions to a new level; to establish a base which can be used as a self-sustaining take-off to further personal growth and action (Young, 1982). The purpose of developing critical knowing is to provide the intellectual tools for individuals themselves to continue in the process of critical reflection without the support of a group leader or other group members, to develop the commitment towards their own critical self-knowing and to have ie skills and tools necessary to achieve it. This is a grand ideal. However, it can be argued that the ideal should be an important aim of many experience-based learning programmes, especially those which are concerned with training and educating learners for decision-making and action. Otherwise learning is not transferred to the work or home situation.

There has not been a great deal of research undertaken into the confronting role of a group leader, although there is an analysis of the stages of intervention (Heron, 1975) and some work on the role behaviours of the critical teacher (Smith, 1978, 1980; Jenks and Murphy, 1978). However, it can be suggested that the group leader in this role would challenge participants as to whether their personal theories (Evers and Walker, 1982) are internally consistent, represent valid claims, reflect the actual world, or are only partial conceptualizations of the 'real' world. For example, a teacher can appear to accept the idea that adults attend educational institutions on a different basis from children — they are voluntary as opposed to compulsory — but still want to continue to exert the same control over the process of learning as in compulsory schooling. Thus the major role of the debriefer within a context aimed at critical knowing is that of a critic, within an atmosphere based upon trust, and relationships of mutual respect for the perceptions and theories of those participating.

Any debriefing session may have aspects of each of these different types of knowledge and ways of knowing. The important issue is that the role and the context for the debriefer and participants should change depending on what outcomes are being sought. If this is not done, conventional knowledge can drown in aimless discussion or checklists and quizzes will cut off the emergence of the interpretative meanings of concepts and issues important to the participants.

The Development of the Skills of Debriefing

From what has been said already it is obvious that the skills necessary for effective debriefing are many and complex. They include structuring and organizing skills, group process skills, communication skills, conflict resolution skills and very often skills in counselling. These skills are not innate but can be developed through formal training and through critical reflection on one's own experience. Anyone who undertakes debriefing episodes without a basic grasp of these skills, or without immediately available skills support from someone else, is placing himself or herself and other participants at risk. As with other skills, however, successful experience in using debriefing skills generates confidence. The level of confidence of a group leader is often reflected in his or her debriefing style.

In preparing this chapter the writers tried to reflect critically on their own development as group leaders of debriefing. Both agreed that initially they sought for and needed control over the debriefing process. On reflection, this need was related to an anxiety concerned with releasing control of the situation, a worry about how participants would react if the writers did relinquish control, and related to this was a lack of confidence in themselves and the skills they needed. We now think that different personalities will feel more comfortable with varying degrees of control and structure. Personalities who need to feel in control will probably feel happier with more structured debriefing. Others who are more comfortable in handling free flowing discussion will feel happy with unstructured debriefing. The main issue is that both styles are legitimate within the context suggested by the types of knowledge outcomes sought for as already discussed. If participants raise issues that the group leader has planned to deal with later in the debriefing process then it is perfectly legitimate to say something like, 'I know that's important to you, but could we come back to that issue later on.'

Such negotiation offers a means to develop a structure, if that is what is needed by the group leader and/or the participants; or the group leader can negotiate the structure and sequence of issues to be covered with the participant group before a debriefing begins. The purpose of this negotiation could well be expressed by the group leader as something like: 'I would feel much more comfortable if we could deal with the issues we want to discuss in some order. I would like to suggest that these should be the issues we deal with. Are there other issues you would like to discuss that I haven't mentioned?'; or issues could be volunteered by participants and group leader, listed and the order for discussion negotiated. Obviously negotiation requires time to make it work effectively. This time must be taken into account when the group leader is planning the programme.

Another possible explanation for the need of some debriefers to keep control of the process, and possibly too why debriefing is often truncated or omitted in experience-based learning, is that the debriefing phase demands a change of style. While the leader organizes an activity there may be a certain god-like quality to the role — *deus ex machina* — but debriefing exposes the leader to questioning, to uncontrolled emotions, divergent and irrelevant ideas. Anything can happen. To take these risks the debriefer needs to have respect for the participants as co-learners, to allow them to share control of the process and trust that their participation is worthwhile in the long term however difficult in the short term.

In their reflection both writers agreed that the first time each of them relinquished control, and found that the learning within the group continued and there were no major repercussions, was an important experience. Sharing power, authority and responsibility for learning, and working towards collaborative learning in debriefing is a satisfying and rewarding process. Both writers now see their debriefing style as more open and flexible, based upon mutual negotiation and collaborative learning. One writer still has some structure in summarizing and drawing issues together at the end of a debriefing phase. However, she thinks this may meet the needs of the participants as well as her own for closure. The participants, their needs and expectations are extremely important factors in any debriefing process. Negotiation as a basis for collaborative learning provides the opportunity for the needs and expectations of all members of the debriefing group to be made explicit and shared (Boomer, 1982).

The Organization of the Debriefing Context

There are many ways to structure the debriefing process. Many people think that formal debriefing should only occur in a large whole group setting. While agreeing that this is probably the norm, there are many arguments for considering the use of individual, pair, and small-group debriefings as well. The following suggestions for the organization of debriefing are given for field experience activities, gaming and simulation activities and for workshop programmes. Each of these is considered to have its own peculiar characteristics which must be taken into account when organizing the debriefing context. In each case whole group debriefing may be impossible, insufficient or only one of a range of possible debriefing structures.

Field Experience
Often the organization of experience-based programmes involves participants working individually at different sites. Because of this a great deal of debriefing may have to occur between the individual and a group leader on site, even though there may also be a later larger group debriefing as well. Rather than being a disadvantage, individually focused debriefing may be extremely effective. For example, it is one writer's experience that to facilitate growth towards critical knowing successfully, where an individual's beliefs about actions are challenged and new planning action, observation and reflection cycles are developed (Carr and Kemmis, 1983), debriefing between a student and himself on site in a specific context is essential and is probably best achieved in a one-to-one relationship.

However, such individual debriefing is best supported by group sessions during or at the end of the programme. The group session allows participants to share their experiences and generalize from the specific experiences. This is the time, too, to evaluate the programme to see how well it met the purposes of the participants and the leader.

Games and Simulations
An issue of importance for gaming and simulation that needs to be distinguished from debriefing is deroling. Deroling means the process of shedding the role taken on for the purpose of an activity and resuming one's usual persona. If deroling does not take place, participants in debriefing may be still reacting in the context of the role they had

79

assumed, rather than attempting to make meaning of the experience as a whole. For example, where participants had roles which involved putting forward conflicting views, they need to stand back from these roles to reflect on how antagonists interact. Individual time to separate from the participant group, sit quietly, go for a walk, and to be alone prior to larger group debriefing, provides time to withdraw from the experience itself, to reflect in a more objective way on feelings and reactions. In some cases it may be necessary to be more explicit and have participants remove labels, badges or costumes and then state how they are different from the persona of their role to achieve disassociation. This deroling may assist in the debriefing and may also help to dispel some anger or frustrations of participants.

Similarly, small group debriefing of participants who have been on the same side or team in a role-play or simulation activity, competing or co-operating with one another, provides the groups with time to reflect upon the experiences of the members of the small group, the roles they played, the manner in which they and other players behaved, and to discuss these things together. It provides an opportunity for each group to consider the goals that were established at the beginning of the activity and whether they succeeded in achieving them. This small group debriefing can assist in deroling participants at the same time. A further important advantage of small group debriefing is that often issues stemming from interpersonal actions which have the potential to arouse anger and conflict in a whole group debriefing can be discussed and dealt with beforehand in the small group debriefing. Thus in a recent experience (Hope and Smith, in press) involving a simulated disaster experience with nurse educators, one of the writers used small group debriefing for both the 'victim' and the 'rescuer' groups prior to their coming together in a final whole group debriefing. Because of this preparatory debriefing many of the actions of the rescuers, which could have caused potentially angry reactions from members of the victims, had already been dealt with by the rescuers. The formal whole group debriefing thus was one of accepting criticism of actions and as a whole group working towards more desirable action alternatives. The level of interpersonal participant anger and conflict in the whole group debriefing was extremely low, largely because of the preparatory small group debriefing.

Prior small group debriefing does have the potential to solidify perceptions of the members of each small group towards other participants. One means to overcome intergroup conflict resulting from this small group identity and solidarity is in arranging the large group for whole group debriefing. Instead of letting members of a particular small group sit together, it may be advisable to intersperse members of different groups. This strategy can break down the feeling of small group unity and solidarity. Combined with having participants remove any evidence of their role as indicated before, it can provide a more individually focused basis for the whole group debriefing.

Workshop Programmes

Individual, small and whole group debriefing can be used for groups such as are usual in the type of workshop style programmes common in staff development and in-service courses. The key feature of these workshops is that a group leader may only work with a group once. Individual reflection may be a particularly useful strategy in one-off programmes as it provides the opportunity to focus on events, actions and reactions. Questionnaires or checklists may provide the substance for larger group debriefing and prompt participants to go deeper in analysing the experience instead of responding at a superficial level in a way that blocks discussion. The use of pairing with or without prior individual reflection is another means to promote this deeper insight. Participants in pairs may ask each other a given set of questions or each listen, without interruption for a set time eg three minutes, to the other telling how he or she feels or reacted to the experience.

Where the whole group is made up of more than about 15 participants, it is often desirable to organize all or most of the debriefing to take place in small groups possibly following individual reflection and/or discussion in pairs. Groups of five or six seem to produce the best results. To be successful the debriefing process needs to be structured clearly with a set of tasks that are self-explanatory and prompt reflection at the level and in the manner required. This is essential because there may not be any contact between the group leader and any single participant, or members of a particular small group, while these tasks are being completed. However, it is desirable to have some form of whole group session before concluding so that overall reactions can be checked and participants can bring up issues they may think have been omitted or underemphasized.

A final important element in organizing debriefing is the use of observers. Many people think that in any experience every participant must be actively involved in the experience itself. There is a great deal to be gained, however, by having a number of observers in a group experience who provide another point of view of what has taken place. Observers should be carefully briefed as to what they are to observe. Different observers may well have different aspects of an activity to observe. Part of their observation may include completing pencil and paper forms indicating the frequency or pattern of a particular action or the actions of a particular group. The observers should then be provided with an opportunity to present their observations at one or more points during the debriefing, maybe working with small groups of participants clarifying perceptions and meanings prior to reporting to the entire group. Similarly, the people who worked with participants on site can also report back on their observations of participants' actions. Observers can have a very powerful and important role in any experience-based activity or learning programme. They provide another source of information and point of view. They can make observations or generalizations that would be seen as negative if coming from the group leader, but which are acceptable from a peer.

Concluding a Debriefing Session

The concluding stage of a debriefing session has a number of purposes. First is that of evaluation. Although the whole debriefing process provides a certain amount of feedback to the debriefer and those who planned the activities as to whether the original intentions of these activities have been realized, feedback is also needed on the value of the activities as a whole from the participants' perspective. Important questions relate to whether participants believe that the experience and the manner in which the activities were structured and organized achieved the original purposes; whether the experience matched participants' beliefs and understandings about the operation of the external world; and whether the outcomes of the experience were useful. Participants can discuss how the activities can be changed so that the participants' experiences more closely approximate the external world and the intentions and expected outcomes of those who planned the event.

This opportunity for evaluation is crucial if the debriefer is attempting to promote critical knowing. If this is the case, the group leader must be prepared for his or her actions and theories to be as open to challenge as are those of the participants, otherwise there is no real sharing and equality.

Second, since debriefing has an important role in the development of group identity and group cohesion, it is important to ensure that at the end of a debriefing process, whether organized on an individual, small group or whole group basis, there are strong positive feelings between the group leader and the participants and among the participants themselves. Levels of anxiety, frustration and injustice should be low and any interpersonal conflict should have been resolved. To achieve this peace at the end of a debriefing session is very important. This is especially so where there is a long-term development of a group, and the need for a positive relationship between the group leader and the participants upon which this development depends. Even in groups which are about to dissolve, often after a short time together, there is a need likewise for any emotion, whether excitement or conflict, to have been addressed.

Finally, there should be a sense that something has been achieved. This can often be gained by the leader outlining briefly where the group has been in the session, giving a brief history of events, restating the purpose of the activities and the major issues discussed. This closure as stressed earlier should be the beginning of further reflection, not the end. As already discussed, the degree of emphasis on closure will reflect both the group leader's and the participants' needs and the group leader's style.

Towards More Effective Debriefing

Debriefing is neither simple nor easy. Effective debriefing relies upon the development of a range of specialized skills. These skills, particularly interpersonal and interventionist skills and the skill of timing, may be developed through deliberate training and are refined through experience; such skills cannot be learnt by reading this or any other chapter. The only way to learn to debrief is by doing it, and by watching others doing it with an attitude of deliberate and critical reflection.

Reflection lies at the core of experience-based learning. Without it, experiences may remain as experiences and the full potential for learning by the participant may not be realized. If debriefing, or some other form of reflective activity, is absent from a programme of experience-based learning, serious questions can be raised concerning that programme's validity and claim to be based in experiential learning. However, ineffective or superficial debriefing may be even worse than no debriefing at all. Effective debriefing depends in part on:

1. A positive commitment to the importance of debriefing and its central role in experience-based learning.
2. The deliberate planning, in any experience-based learning activity, for an adequate opportunity for debriefing to occur.
3. A realization that effective debriefing depends upon a high level of facilitatory skill and a determination by those who facilitate debriefing to either possess, or develop these skills.
4. The establishment of clear intentions, objectives and purposes for activities which are conveyed to participants during the briefing phase and which, with the debriefing, form the framework within which the activities take place.
5. The identification of the ways of knowing and types of knowledge which any experience represents and the establishment of appropriate context, structures and relationships in which any debriefing process will take place.
6. The establishment of a debriefing environment based upon trust, acceptance, willingness to take risks and the mutual respect of individuals' feelings, perceptions and theories.

If these simple but essential rules are followed and supported by a skilful and sensitive group leader, then debriefing, which as a form of reflection is the key to successful experience-based learning, can be highly effective. Debriefing is an area of experience-based learning that is central yet about which there is much more to be discovered. It therefore demands a high priority for further research and investigation.

References

Boomer, G (1982) *Negotiating the Curriculum*, Gosford, NSW: Ashton Scholastics

Carr, W and Kemmis, S (1983) *Becoming Critical: Knowing Through Action Research*, Geelong, Victoria: Deakin University Press

Evers, C and Walker, J (1982) The unity of knowledge, *Access*, 1, 2 pp33-54

Habermas, J (1971) *Knowledge and Human Interest*, Boston, Mass: Beacon

Habermas, J (1974) *Theory and Practice*, London: Heinemann

Harvey, L V (1979) Small groups and essential learning, *Australian Journal of Adult Education*, 14, 1, pp21-26

Heron, J (1975) *Six Category Intervention Analysis*, Guildford, Surrey: Centre for Adult Education, University of Surrey

Hirst, P (1974) *Knowledge and the Curriculum, a Collection of Philosophical Papers*, London: Routledge and Kegan Paul

Hope, J and Smith, D (in press) *Experience-based Learning in Nursing Education: a Simulated Disaster*

Jenks, C and Murphy, C (1978) *Overview to Experience-based Learning and the Facilitative Role of the Teacher*, San Francisco, California: Far West Laboratory for Educational Research and Development

Johnson, D (1972) *Reaching Out*, New Jersey: Prentice Hall

Jones, R M|(1968) *Fantasy and Feeling in Education*, New York: New York University Press

Kemmis, S, Cole, P and Suggett, D (1983) *Towards the Socially Critical School*, Melbourne: Victorian Institute of Secondary Education

McCarthy, J and Easby, M (1983) Training RAF instructors in the skills of briefing, monitoring and debriefing, using microteaching methodologies, in Trott, A, Strongman, H and Giddins, L (eds) *Improving Efficiency in Education and Training, Aspects of Educational Technology XVI*, London: Kogan Page

Mulford, B (1977) *Structured Experiences for Use in the Classroom*, Canberra: Centre for Continuing Education, Australian National University

Pfeiffer, J W and Jones, E J (1975) *A Handbook of Structured Experiences for Human Relations Training, Vol 1*, La Jolla, California: University Associates Inc

Phenix, P (1964) *Realms of Meaning*, New York: McGraw-Hill

Schwab, J (1964) The structure of disciplines: meanings and significances, in Ford, G and Pugno, L (eds) *The Structure of Knowledge and the Curriculum*, Chicago, Illinois: Rand McNally, pp1-30

Smith, D (1978) Some current problems of teaching practice, in Smith, D, Williams, G and Watson, G *School-based Teacher Education: Reports on Two Sydney Innovations*, Sydney: Department of Education, University of Sydney, Occasional Paper, No 2, pp1-19

Smith, D (1980) School-based teacher education: new practicum relationships between school and teacher education institutions, in *The Role of School Experience in Teacher Education: Recent Trends and Future Developments*, Armidale: Collected papers of a national conference, pp127-136

Smith, D (1981) Briefing and debriefing, *Journal of the Australian Decision, Simulation and Educational Gaming Association* (ADSEGA), pp1-18

van Ments, M (1983) *The Effective Use of Role-play: a Handbook for Teachers and Trainers*, London: Kogan Page

Watson, H J, Vallee, J M and Mulford, W R (1981) *Structured Experiences and Group Development*, Canberra: Curriculum Development Centre

Young, R (1982) Critical theory, curriculum and teaching, *Discourse*, 3, 1, pp22-39

CHAPTER 5
Reflection and Learning: the Importance of a Listener

Susan Knights, *Adult Learning Consultant, Sydney*

Reflection as a mental process is usually thought of as an internal activity, carried out in solitude, for which the presence of other people is often an unwelcome distraction. In the physical world, however, reflection is a two-way process; without an appropriate 'reflector' it cannot occur at all. In this chapter I shall argue that, in the learning situation, reflection is most profound when it is done aloud with the aware attention of another person.

My own experience of the value of another person's attention comes from the practice of co-counselling in which two people who have received training in the techniques of peer counselling take turns to counsel each other (Heron, 1973).

I became involved in co-counselling after experiencing several other kinds of personal growth activities which, although stimulating and rewarding in many ways, had an important drawback in that they depended on the presence of a leader and a group of participants who waited, or competed, for their turn for the leader's attention (a situation with obvious parallels in the traditional learning group). The attraction of co-counselling was that it offered me the chance of learning to assist other people in their personal exploration and to pursue my own in a continuing reciprocal process whereby I could meet as often as I liked with another co-counsellor and spend half the time giving them my attention and half the time using their attention for whatever I wanted to work on.

Although many aspects of my experience with co-counselling and its distinctive theory of human development (Jackins, 1978) have proved invaluable in my work in adult education the particular technique which is relevant here is the simplest of all, that of placing all of one's attention and awareness at the disposal of another person, listening with interest and appreciation without interrupting or engaging in discussion. This is known as giving free attention. It sounds like a very simple process, and it is, but it is also surprisingly powerful:

> Free attention is the facilitating energy of awareness. Giving free attention is an intense activity, a fundamental validation of the person to whom it is given. (Heron, 1974)

Receiving someone's undivided attention is also a rare experience. We spend a great deal of our waking time talking to each other and many teachers and group leaders will say, 'I often get my students to pair up and talk to each other.' Talking is common; what is far less common and far harder to obtain is good listening.

Harvey Jackins, the major theorist of the form of co-counselling known as re-evaluation counselling, has spoken of the problem as follows:

> If you think back to the coffee shop or picnic table or similar situations you will remember that people are, everywhere and at all times in the presence of each other, either trying to be listened to – talking every chance they get – or waiting impatiently for a chance to interrupt any other person who is talking and start talking themselves. You will find that whenever people are together, they're making an effort to be listened to, and *are* very seldom listened to because the person that they are trying to get to listen to them is waiting desperately and impatiently for a chance to be listened to himself or herself. (Jackins, 1983, p173)

In the traditional learning situation the only person who has a real opportunity to talk without interruption is the teacher; students may ask questions or answer them and perhaps engage in discussion with each other but such discussions, however well facilitated, involve competition for a space to speak and very rarely the chance to follow through a train of thought in a thorough way without distraction. One initial disadvantage of my experience with co-counselling was that as I grew accustomed to enjoying sessions of full attention from my co-counsellors, I found that my capacity to give attention to others (not just my counselling partners) increased enormously. I found that in groups I would automatically focus on whoever started talking and give them my complete attention. This naturally encouraged them to continue at length, useful for them in unravelling their thoughts about whatever our topic was, but frustrating for everyone else. The obvious solution was to organize things so that the students could listen to each other, with the ground rule of no interruptions, especially not criticism, for an equal and limited amount of time.

Although the rules about no interrupting and sharing time equally may seem restrictive and artificial, they actually provide a great sense of freedom for both speaker and listener. The talker can concentrate on pursuing his or her argument at a comfortable pace without worrying about forestalling interruptions, answering questions or being entertaining to the listeners to hold their attention, and the listeners can give unqualified attention without any worry about 'How long is this going on?' or 'How am I going to get my word in?' because they know that their time will come. At the same time, because the subject matter is of mutual interest, they can benefit from listening to their partners' thoughts as well as sorting out their own.

One-to-one Listening in Practice

The most detailed and helpful account I have discovered of using this process in a learning situation is David Potts' chapter in *Developing Student Autonomy in Learning* (1981). In this paper Potts describes how he taught a course on Mexican history at La Trobe University in a series of three-hour workshops which included regular opportunities for one-to-one talking on specific questions set by the lecturer. An example from the first workshop is the question, 'What is a fact?' which the students had to answer for three minutes each, followed by a second 'round' of three minutes each and then time for general group discussion.

The students were asked to submit a 500-word report on each workshop in the form of a journal and these provided useful feedback about the students' reaction to the technique. At first they were uneasy:

> I felt some unease at being drawn, nay forced, into conversation with a total stranger. (Potts, 1981, p101)

but many comments indicated that being 'forced' to think aloud without fear of interruption was a very positive experience:

> The talker can 'confront' the listener with ideas of his own without fear of being knocked back or laughed at (and thus becoming defensive), reaching conclusions he may not otherwise have reached. (Potts, 1981, p102)

> It was very big to know you could throw it in and kick it around and not get shouted down. Maybe it is real security blanket stuff, but it certainly encouraged some original thought. (Potts, 1981, p102)

In the course described by Potts one-to-one talking without interruption had a central position in the course design. However, it might be difficult for anyone who has not experienced the value of this kind of exchange in an activity like co-counselling to adopt it in such a major fashion. It is important, therefore, to point out that although the guidelines about sharing time equally and listening without interruption need to be applied rigidly the activity may be introduced in a variety of ways as shown in the following examples taken from contributions to the re-evaluation counselling journals *Colleague* and *Classroom*:

> I give short clear explanations of major points, usually talking not longer than ten to fifteen minutes without a break for some other activity. Then people turn to their talking partners and give their reactions to the ideas we are discussing. The room always roars pleasantly with fifteen to twenty pairs of talkers. (Huse, 1977, p38)

> Breaking up into twos and threes with individuals I had never met was enjoyable. It became so easy to ramble on and on with people listening so intently. I can see how this would make you feel good about yourself and therefore better able to learn. (Carr, 1980, p66)

> One of my favourite gimmicks is to give the class pairs of problems that illustrate a point that I am making and then to ask people to pair up, not always with the same person. First one, then the other works out one of the problems, telling out loud what s/he is doing at each step. By forcing the person who is doing the problem to state explicitly what s/he is doing, people cannot pretend a non-existent understanding of the problem. I have people work together in their seats where they are safe by themselves. (Jackins, 1983, p29)

One-to-one attention has even been used in practical art courses:

> I required drawing students to create in pairs, one watching the other draw. The watcher noted in writing the step by step development of images. Roles were then reversed and information exchanged. One woman reported she had never seen a drawing being done or thought about its progression. Insights were numerous; most students asked for more. (Keller, 1978, p64)

Two things strike me in particular about the students' comments quoted above; they speak of 'insights', 'original thoughts' and 'conclusions he may not otherwise have reached', all of which indicate effective reflection, and they appreciate the safety of being able to think aloud without fear of critical or sarcastic comment, 'without fear of being knocked back or laughed at'. I believe that this safety plays an essential part in promoting reflection. Carl Rogers has written that:

> My experience in psychotherapy leads me to believe that by setting up conditions of psychological safety and freedom, we maximise the likelihood of an emergence of constructive creativity. (Rogers, 1961, p357)

My experience in co-counselling as well as working with groups of students has convinced me that very few people, however highly qualified academically, have confidence in their capacity to think. The fear of being 'knocked back or laughed at' is very widespread. This certainly inhibits participation in group discussion and, in my view, also discourages private reflection.

Why should this be? It seems likely that we were all born with a questioning and reflective nature; the constant and sometimes bizarre questions of young people, once they learn to speak, strongly suggests that they are constantly observing and reflecting on all that goes on around them. The experience of formal schooling unfortunately tends to have a dampening effect on this enthusiasm; instead of one or more reasonably attentive adults willing to listen to the observations and answer the questions generated there is one teacher whose attention has to be shared and competed for with 20 or 30 others. Speaking aloud becomes much less safe, both asking and answering questions leaves the student potentially vulnerable. Even if a teacher wishes to encourage students to respect their own thinking, the system is loaded against this when success comes from performance judged by the standards of an external authority.

Hence the value of the opportunity to think aloud with another person's respectful attention and no threat of interruption. However much the process may start by feeling stilted and artificial the effect is to provide a valuable contradiction to the feeling, 'My thinking isn't worth listening to.' In my experience this is demonstrated by the fact that students not only appear to enjoy their one-to-one sessions but also, in a course which continues from week to week, they begin to speak out more confidently in group discussions.

As well as this important increase in confidence, speaking to an interested listener also has the advantage of keeping students' attention on the topic, something which is much harder to do when a group leader simply says, 'Just take a few minutes to think about this yourselves.' On the other hand the one-to-one sessions may sometimes be useful as a chance for students to let off steam, to complain about the irritating mannerisms of a lecturer, obnoxious behaviour from fellow students or worry aloud about a dental appointment at the end of the day. None of these is relevant to subject matter but no worthwhile reflection is likely to take place while they are at the forefront of the learner's mind and, while I am not suggesting that the classroom or lecture theatre is an appropriate place for a full scale counselling session, a few moments grumbling to a sympathetic listener can often be enough to allow consideration of the topic to proceed more fruitfully.

Even when interruptions are not critical or sarcastic they can have the effect of inhibiting thinking. Writing about co-counselling, psychologist Jerome Liss stresses the powerful effect of receiving uninterrupted attention, and, like Harvey Jackins, points out how seldom it is available:

> One of the reasons co-counselling works is that it sets the stage for un-interrupted attention given to one person. Uninterrupted attention is an essential human need and helps the working out of any problem. One of the reasons spouses and friends so often fail to help one another is that they are inclined to interrupt. Not just an interrupting remark, although this itself can break the delicate thread of a talker's stream of consciousness and feeling, but just to interrupt the talker's point of attention can botch up the job. An uncalled for interpretation or unasked for advice will often do this. Even worse is 'This happened to me too . . .' (Liss, 1974, p205)

In a statement quoted by David Potts in the paper cited above, Liss goes further and suggests that the experience of constant interruption makes it hard for us to sustain reflective thinking even when alone:

> Repetitive interruptions not only chop up the ongoing stream of thoughts and feelings of the moment but the two person pattern is internalised and repeated by the interrupted person's mind when alone. (Potts, 1981, p95)

If that is the case then perhaps the regular experience of receiving uninterrupted attention can lead to improved concentration even without the presence of a listener.

Effect on the Role of the Teacher or Group Leader

When students are engaging in one-to-one listening, the role of the teacher undergoes a dramatic transformation. From being the centre of attention, he or she is reduced to a timekeeper. It is important for the successful implementation of the activity that the leader can tolerate this abrupt change. Potts' description of his first course conducted in this way includes the comment that, although he believed that what the students were doing was valuable, he found the feeling of being superfluous while the one-to-one sessions were under way somewhat disturbing:

> For the great part, however, the immediate experience was, as I said, one of lost control, lost authority. (Potts, 1981, p99)

He later suggests that colleagues who tried the method on the basis of reading about it (or recommendations from Potts' students) without personal experience of its benefits ran into difficulties with this loss of control and found the activity less than impressive because they did not promote it wholeheartedly, did not encourage their students to believe in it, or take the ground rules seriously.

It is also true that some students find the exercise hard, especially at first and if the one-to-one exchange is introduced in a large group in a situation such as a lecture a number of the participants will tend to disregard the guidelines and engage in a conversation. However, as indicated by the comments quoted above and my own experience in using this process in a variety of learning situations, most will benefit from it.

When it is taken seriously by both learners and teachers I believe that the simple technique of asking students to pair up and take equal amounts of time listening to each other as they think aloud is the best possible way of ensuring that reflection is included in the learning process. For the reasons discussed above, talking through one's ideas with the thoughtful attention of another person is a powerful way of clarifying confusion, identifying appropriate questions and reaching significant insights. Argument, evaluation and constructive feedback also have their place in the process of course, along with lectures, reading, group discussion and practical experience, but much of their value can be lost without the opportunity for all students to process the input in their own way, check it against previously acquired information and make it their own.

References

Carr, S (1980) *Classroom*, 7, Seattle: Rational Island Publishers

Heron, J (1973) Re-evaluation counselling: personal growth through mutual aid, *British Journal of Guidance and Counselling*, 1, 2

Heron, J (1974) *Reciprocal Counselling Manual*, Human Potential Research Project, University of Surrey

Huse, D (1977) *Colleague*, 2, Seattle: Rational Island Publishers

Jackins, H (1978) *The Human Side of Human Beings: the Theory of Re-evaluation Counselling*, Seattle: Rational Island Publishers

Jackins, H (1983) *The Reclaiming of Power*, Seattle: Rational Island Publishers

Jackins, T (1977) *Colleague*, 2, Seattle: Rational Island Publishers

Keller, F (1978) *Colleague*, 3, Seattle: Rational Island Publishers

Liss, J (1974) *Free to Feel*, London: Wildwood House

Potts, D (1981) One-to-one learning, in Boud, D J (ed) *Developing Student Autonomy in Learning*, London: Kogan Page, pp94-112

Rogers, C R (1961) *On Becoming a Person*, Boston: Houghton Mifflin

CHAPTER 6
Reflection and the Development of Learning Skills

Alex Main, *University of Strathclyde*

Learning to learn has been the subject of much attention in the last decade in secondary and post-secondary education. There has been a substantial movement away from the rather rigid study methods manuals of the 1950s and 1960s towards more experiential and more reflective activities which involve learners in a monitoring and evaluating of their own learning capacities and styles. This shift may owe something to the emphasis placed by Michael Oakeshott on practical knowledge — 'organised abilities to discern, to judge and to perform' (Oakeshott, 1962). These abilities, he suggests, are so rooted in our understanding, beliefs, values and attitudes that any 'rules' we try to apply to our learning would be inadequate and partial expressions of what is involved.

In stressing the importance of 'knowing how', Oakeshott says:

> Facts, rules, all that may come to us as information, itemised and explicit, never themselves endow us with an ability to do, or to make, or to understand and explain anything . . . rules are always disjunctive. They specify only an act or a conclusion of a certain general kind and they never relieve us of the necessity of choice. (Oakeshott, 1968)

A lot of recent work on learning skills has stressed this element of personal choice about learning styles and methods. Much of it is aimed at making students' learning more accessible to scrutiny and reflection and more available for decision and change. Two examples where individuals are encouraged to examine their own learning are my own work (Main, 1980) and that of Graham Gibbs (1981). My approach involves the mediation of an individual teacher or counsellor as an agent of reflection. Gibbs has devised situations and exercises which mobilize the reflective strength of groups of learners to assist each other. Both stem from concern about the inadequacy of standard 'cook-books' on methods of study and about the overrigid rules often culled from psychology and educational theory (see especially Gibbs, 1981, pp60-65; Main, 1983).

Let me describe the rationale which Graham Gibbs puts forwards for his methods. He points out that there is very little evidence for a clear, strong relationship between study habits and academic success and yet the text books and programmes on study methods do advocate general study techniques in the hope that they will improve student learning. He argues that giving advice in a generalized way without regard to the individual student or course or method of assessment is not very likely to have a

positive effect. What, he asks, happens when you tell people how to learn?
What is the effect of giving advice? What is the effect of suggesting rules
that they might follow? His answer is that by and large the advice is not
acted upon. Some advice looks impossible for the student to take because
it lacks an understanding of the process of student learning. Some advice
is impossible to take because what is described is impossible. Some advice
involves a threatening attack on the existing ways that students have of
doing things. His most important telling point, however, is that some
advice does not lead to any change even when it is accepted by students.
He suggests that there are several ways that this happens, all of them
emphasizing some aspect of the difference between knowing how to do
something and actually doing it.

> Students often have rationalizations for their study habits which bear little
> relationship to what they actually do. As I have already mentioned students
> often claim that the reason they take notes is to revise from them afterwards
> but they *do not* often revise from them because this can be such a dull and
> profitless activity. While attempting to teach students how to study through a
> National Extension College course my students were required to send me
> their notes from a chapter of the course text which covered note taking.
> A good proportion of these students had copied out, word for word, the
> advice in the text always to take notes in one's own words. Also, some had
> copied advice to structure notes in one's own way and use one's own headings,
> and had embedded this advice in notes laid out, structured, and headed
> *exactly* as in the chapter. Clearly these students had learnt the advice, at
> some level, without it influencing their study in any way (Gibbs, 1981, p67)

Clearly Gibbs is suggesting that these students lack any proper reflection
on their learning, and the exercises which he has designed are an attempt
to develop such reflection. He suggests there are six interrelated ways
to facilitate students' learning development.

1. Take a student centred approach.
2. Give responsibility to the student for his or her own learning.
3. Make change of methods and approaches a safe activity.
4. Emphasize the student's purpose not technique.
5. Emphasize the reconceptualization of study tasks.
6. Emphasize the student's awareness of his or her own learning.

In this list quite clearly 5. and 6. are the root of reflective activity. Let me
illustrate this in practice by showing one of Graham Gibbs' practical
exercises in learning. I have chosen his exercise 'How do we learn best?'
which is designed to act as an initial impetus to students thinking about
their own learning. Gibbs suggests that it works well as an initial
orientation for srudents to pay attention to and value their own
experience of learning.

Instructions

Working alone (3 min): 'Think back to some past experience of learning —
it could be at school, in sports, in a hobby, anything that was particularly
awful — it may have been boring or humiliating or you simply learnt

nothing at all. Jot down a few notes on why it was so bad.'
(3 min): 'Now do the same for a good learning experience — where
you learnt a lot, were successful, enjoyed it and were interested. What
was it that made learning so good? Jot down a few notes.'

Working pairs (10 min): 'Relate your experiences to each other, in pairs.
Explain why your experiences were good or bad. What are the main
similarities between what makes learning good or bad for you both? In
what ways do you seem to thrive or suffer in different circumstances?
Try and stick to basing your discussion in your own personal experiences
rather than generalizing.'

Working in fours (24 min): 'Form a group of four with another pair. From
your pooled experiences of good and bad learning, can you see any themes
arising — things which for you tend to characterize good and bad learning
in general? Each group of four elects a chairman who notes down what is
said under two columns: "Things that lead to unsatisfactory learning"
and "Things that tend to support and encourage very satisfactory
learning." Note down as many things as you can under these headings.'

Working in plenary (20 min): 'I'd like each group of four, in turn, to read
out one item from its list. I'd like everyone else to ask that group to
explain itself, to make the meaning of each item clear. Also, for each
item, I'd like suggestions as to how that might affect the way you are
learning here, in this institution, now.'

Continue until items or time are exhausted.

Gibbs suggests that this exercise helps students to discover what they
already know from their own experience about 'good' learning and about
what they themselves can do to bring about improvements in learning.
To this extent he is advocating that reflective techniques allow individual
development, individual choice and a matching of learning methods and
study techniques to individual needs and perceptions. Incidentally, I have
used the same exercise with teaching staff in a number of British
universities and have found it an excellent base from which to develop
the teaching skills and perceptions of academics. The reflection required
in the exercise seems to allow teachers to link their own teaching
behaviour with the values that they place on their own learning.

This concept of value in teaching and learning links to my own work
in study counselling. Where Graham Gibbs has developed reflection
through group activity, I have been concerned to improve the reflective
activity of individual students through the counselling process. My work
relates quite closely to the work of Raths *et al* (1966, 1967) and his work
in the areas of valuing and thinking. Among the skills which Raths and
his followers have suggested are required by effective teachers is the skill
of evoking expressions of judgement and that of clarifying the student's
judgement procedures. One whole set of procedures for clarifying is
labelled by Raths the reflective mode. This mode involves such things as:

1. Saying back exactly what the student has said but with an inflection indicating that a question has been raised.
2. Paraphrasing the student's remarks saying 'Did I understand you?', followed by the paraphrase comment.
3. Requesting the student to expand his or her views saying 'Tell me more'.
4. Soliciting statements from the student asking 'Is this close to your life right now?'
5. Relating feelings and behaviour asking 'Tell me how you felt when you . . .?'

I believe that all methods of counselling employ just such reflective techniques. Counselling involves three phased activities. First listening and exploring, then understanding and relating, and finally focusing and assisting.

These three are essential stages in assisting an individual to reflect. Listening gives an opportunity to individuals to express themselves — all human beings need time to express themselves — even the most articulate people cannot sum up how they feel or how they perceive a situation in a few minutes. Exploration is an extended form of listening, but it is an active form of listening — using questions which turn back people's statements to themselves, thus helping them to see just what statements they are making. The act of understanding and relating is one in which individuals are given some sense of solidarity or reassurance, their self image or sense of worth is actively supported, the discoveries they are beginning to make about their own judgement, their own values, their own behaviour are given some credibility through the other person. In focusing, the counsellor recognizes that solutions to problems do not reside within himself or herself but within the students — they stem from the students' own thinking and that thinking must be recognized by them if it is to be acceptable. When it comes to assisting, that assistance is offered in a reflective fashion. The counsellor helps by becoming a focus for the decision-making that students have to make — helps students to move from uncertainty towards a course of action of their own choosing. Or it may be that the counsellor can become an information source providing sensible methods, useful skills for achieving the new targets that have been set by students through reflection on their own needs, their own behaviour, their own problems.

Let me illustrate the way in which counselling can help students reflect upon their approach to two of the basic skills of being a student. First, planning study time and second, notetaking.

There is a lot of information available on methods of time-tabling — ways of using study time more effectively. All the general text books on how to study contain sections on these topics and there are several publications solely devoted to them. The difficulty which faces the student is not that of getting information or advice but applying it in his or her own life. The teacher's difficulty is in ensuring that the student adequately expresses and explores any problem of time. To many students the organization of work looks as if it ought to be very straightforward. When they find themselves budgeting their time unwisely or having difficulty in working effectively then they find it hard to describe what is happening to them. Many seem afraid to admit that they are falling down on the elementary skills of the job. Sitting down with an interested other person — whether that person is called teacher or counsellor — and painting a picture of the world in words, diagrams or lists can be an excellent way for students to find a perspective on time. The teacher or counsellor can encourage students to describe their formal commitments to the college or to family and friends; to describe activities on which they place some value and know they would not wish to reduce in any way; to describe ways in which they depend on other people, or other people depend on them; to outline ways in which they try to satisfy their own physical, emotional, spiritual needs and so on. In this way the manner in which the student has developed a particular lifestyle can be explored. Conflicts between elements of that lifestyle can be highlighted. Students can begin to see how the way in which they organize or do not organize parts of their day produces psychological barriers and blocks to study. They can begin to realize that there are activities which increase and those which decrease their motivation to work. All of these are insights through reflecting on time, reflecting on how it is used and reflecting on the reordering of it. Students who are encouraged to undertake reflection of this kind may not become more 'organized' students but they are likely to become students who are aware of the demands on their time and aware of the way in which study fits into their personal lifestyle. To that extent they will be more confident students at the end of the day. Confidence probably relates as much to success as does effective study method.

The same kind of reflection can be encouraged in relation to specific study skills — notetaking from books and lectures is a good example. Students who enter higher education are seldom given any help with the skill of taking notes even though they spend a significant amount of their time in the university or college in situations where notetaking is required. They are almost always left to develop the skill by trial and error. Effective notetaking is a boon to students — it can help them to pay attention to what they are reading or listening to and it can aid their understanding of material. This second is achieved if students can find ways of coding new information in a way which will integrate it into their existing framework of knowledge. Students seem to appreciate this for they seldom come to their teachers to complain about not taking enough notes, but about taking 'bad' notes. The help that they look for is in identifying ways in which their notes are inadequate and how they can set about making them more systematic and organized.

The most significant help that the teacher or counsellor can give to students is through inviting them to reflect on the purpose of taking notes in the first place. Many students have not, however, explored the range of reasons why they take notes from books or lectures. Most do so because it is a common student activity, almost as if it were expected of them. First the students have to come to terms with the fact that their notes are not a transcript of events or ideas but that they can serve, at some later date, as a revision aid or an *aide-mémoire* in an examination situation or in a practical setting. Then the concept of organization of notes to match that purpose becomes much easier to evolve, the nature of summarizing, of highlighting,|of headlining and all the other specific skills of effective notetaking begin to match a real purpose and are not simply rules to be followed in order to have 'better' notes. Thus notetaking becomes a purposeful activity and one which matches aims and needs enlisted from the students themselves. Further details of counselling techniques in relation to specific skills such as notetaking, essay writing, examination revision, reading, etc, are given in Main (1980).

It is too easy to describe counselling in such a way that the whole process sounds mechanistic. Becoming involved with another person, and becoming a significant 'other' to that person is not achieved by following rules or rehearsing set patterns of behaviour. Listening is a dynamic activity: it is a different experience for each different voice and each different idea expressed by that voice. Relating is dynamic: it develops qualitatively and you cannot reckon it in terms of threshold amounts. Assisting is dynamic: the relationship between two people orchestrates a pattern of assistance, not an inventory. It is the dynamism of interaction which makes for uncertainty — and which can create problems for the effectiveness of a counselling relationship.

As far as I can make out from my experience in counselling learners, there are three key issues which affect the strength of relationships and which can 'threaten' the skills of the counsellor. These three issues relate to the establishment of reflective activities.

Opening Up
The initial stages of any relationship can serve as a model for much of its future development. Just as an authoritarian first lesson in the classroom can inhibit students from expressing their own opinions in later class-meetings, so can a first exchange between counsellor and counsellee foster or inhibit the growth of reflection. I try in every first meeting to encourage positively an act of reflection. This may be to ask the student to write down a 'diary item', thought or feeling about our meeting, which he or she can read just before coming back next time. Or it may be to ask the student to write me a short letter after leaving, telling me what issues came up in our original meeting. It could be that I invite the learner to write a fictitious note to a past teacher, telling that person what feelings have been left over from previous learning experiences. I might even ask the student to script a short dialogue with a present teacher who features strongly in a difficult course. A great deal depends upon the willingness of the student, the verbal fluency and the expressive capacity he or she seems to display. What is important is that the learner is encouraged to employ a communicative technique of some sort to express a feeling or

thought which originates from within — and not merely to describe external conditions or consequences. I may be influenced in this by my own past experience in the use of painting as a therapy with disturbed adolescents — 'Paint me a feeling or draw me a thought'.

Creating Self-concepts

Some learners are over-conscious of the 'otherness' of knowledge, of the external nature of the subject they are studying. What they have to learn originates outside of themselves — in a teacher, a book or a television programme. They regard themselves as vessels into which information and knowledge are poured. They seem to sense themselves as vehicles for the replication and perpetuation of what is 'taught' to them. These students are often rote-learners because they have little confidence in internalizing or 'owning' their learning — or little experience of so doing.

There are also learners, however, who seem to have no personal basis for judgements of the worth of their learning, or for judgements of success or failure in learning. They seem to be unable to predict confidently the consequences of different study methods or learning styles. It is as if they believe that success or failure is determined by external agents — using inscrutable criteria.

Both these groups of students need help in comparing different forms of learning. If they can be helped to make direct comparisons they seem to become more open to reflection on their own role in learning. I try with such students to involve them in some simple exercises which start off not unlike the Graham Gibbs group exercise 'How do we learn best?' which is described above. The student may be asked to think back to a situation in the past when learning seemed less structured, less rigid — or when it was a more adventurous experience; or to think about the present — about differences between learning in college and, for example, picking up skills at a sport or acquiring new ideas in a hobby. Anywhere, in fact, where comparisons can be drawn.

This is not a quick process: it can mean many meetings, successively encouraging the student to move closer and closer to personal experience and further and further from the external, impersonal forces in learning. It means reinforcing by any means — verbal ones, non-verbal gestures of interest — any statement of personal commitment, value, opinion or involvement in decisions about learning. It is not until the rote-learner or the 'fatalistic' learner conceives of self-in-learning that the reflection process can really take place.

Developing Trust in Reflection

If reflection comes slowly to some people because they have little sense of involvement in their own learning, it comes unwillingly to others because they have little belief in its value for them. There are people who find it difficult to reflect on their learning because when they have done so in the past they have not found it a rewarding experience. Maybe for some people all forms of introspection are coloured by unpleasant experiences of looking inward at their own emotions. Maybe for some an examination of learning processes has been an empty experience: nothing of consequence was noticed, nothing worth remarking upon. It could be for some that all their reflection has been done for them by others — overbearing parents may have told them what they think and feel (or should think and feel).

I do not know enough about the limitations experienced by such individuals: all I know is that I can very often strongly sense in some people a great resistance to any form of reflection on their educational experience. Nor can I offer any ideal way of coping with this lack of trust in reflection. I have to admit to relying on chance developments in all that I have done in the past with those who resist reflecting. By offering students an enormous number of opportunities to reflect — by offering opportunities for comparing past and present or different qualities of experience, by assisting them to examine their relationship with me or with tutors, by helping them write down stray thoughts, and so on — I have usually found something that has triggered a rewarding experience. Simply persevering in the setting up of opportunities for reflection has worked: maybe I have randomly chanced upon an appropriate trigger — perhaps a little like finding the elusive cue to speech in the traumatic aphasic patient.

It is very frustrating to have to admit to having no explanation other than saying 'Everyone will have something they can safely and satisfyingly reflect about and you need to keep helping until you both find it.' That is all I can say, however, at this point in my experience.

If students can be encouraged to reflect on their learning with confidence and ease, then there are many likely benefits. It would take a whole book of case studies to illustrate these: the student whose choice of course was made by dominating parents or teachers and who begins to see his or her own potential for choosing and deciding; the student who chose a factual subject because it was easy to rote-learn and who begins to realize that he or she gets so much more personal challenge from those subjects which use problem-solving skills; the adult learner who chose a university course for its prestige value and who willingly transfers to a vocational college course with more direct feedback and personal guidance support services; and the housewife returning to study who develops greater awareness of the source of guilt feelings about changes in the household's standards. These benefits are not to be measured on any absolute scale, but in terms of the new (or renewed) freedom of choice experienced by the learner.

Many students are under pressure from the outside world to accept the values and opinions of elders and betters, teachers or advisers, parents or spouses, subject specialists and potential employers. To them there is a low apparent value to their own inner world. Counselling, which aims to give added credibility to that personal work and bestow ownership in interaction with the world of learning, increases that value.

The counselling approach and the Gibbs group approach have in common an aim of encouraging students:

A questioning and self analytical attitude to their own learning strategies which can continue to be of use to them as their studying develops. This contrasts with the giving of advice and the training in specific techniques where students remain dependent on further inputs from experts to bring about further change. Learning to learn is not a one stage process. Interventions do not bring about immediate changes in study effectiveness . . . the design of such interventions must take into account the fact that learning to learn is a continuous lifelong process. (Gibbs and Northedge, 1979)

In that vein it is worth remembering that many activities under the heading of evaluation of teaching are in themselves opportunities for reflection by learners and can be used to focus learners on to the process of their own learning as well as the outcome of it. Questions directed at learners at the end of a course or the end of a single learning experience can be reflective in nature: 'What do you remember of the course?', 'What strikes you now as the most significant parts of the course you have just completed?', 'What did you learn from this experience?', 'How did that learning come about?', 'What did you do as a result of that learning?'

These are questions which in their various forms as open-ended questions or scaled items in a questionnaire encourage learners to examine the process and content of learning. They are part of the whole repertory of reflective techniques which helps with the development of learning skills: reflection on the learning process or on learning styles, reflection on the teaching process or on the source of learning difficulties, reflection on one's own motivation or on one's personal skills — these are activities which are designed to ensure that learners learn in a meaningful way.

References

Gibbs, G (1981) *Teaching Students to Learn: A Student Centred Approach*, Milton Keynes: Open University Press

Gibbs, G and Northedge, A (1979) Helping students to understand their own study methods, *British Journal of Guidance and Counselling*, 7, pp91-100

Main, A (1980) *Encouraging Effective Learning*, Edinburgh: Scottish Academic Press

Main, A (1983) The improvement of study, in Zuber-Skerritt, O (ed) *Video in Higher Education*, London: Kogan Page

Oakeshott, M (1962) *Rationalism in Politics*, London: Methuen

Oakeshott, M (1968) Learning and teaching, in Peters, R S (ed)*The Concept of Education*, London: Routledge & Kegan Paul

Raths, L E, Harmin, M and Simon, S B (1966) *Values and Teaching*, Columbus, Ohio: Charles E Merrill

Raths, L E, Jonas, A, Rothstein, A and Wasserman, S (1967) *Teaching for Thinking*, Columbus, Ohio: Charles E Merrill

CHAPTER 7
Reflection and the Self-organized Learner: a Model of Learning Conversations

Philip Candy, *University of British Columbia*
Sheila Harri-Augstein, *Brunel University*
Laurie Thomas, *Brunel University*

Introduction

An Australian television advertisement depicts a well known Australian cricketer extolling the virtues of a particular brand of portable video recorder and camera. 'With this', he says, 'I can pick up a batsman's weaknesses *and* improve my bowling action.' What a difference films (and, more recently, videos) have made to sports coaching! Years ago, sports performances could be improved only through repeated practice, with the aid of an observer (generally a coach) who would identify weaknesses and have the competitor practise to overcome the problem. Now, instead of relying on secondhand accounts of their performances, people are able to obtain direct records of their behaviour; they can observe their action, play it and replay it, slow it down or speed it up, compare examples of their style in widely differing situations and generally observe their own behaviour with a degree of objectivity and detachment. The benefit of this is enormous — for the competitor is able to reflect on his or her own performance and, through reflection, improve it.

Sports coaching is by no means the only arena where students can benefit from feedback on their behaviours as they engage in learning activities: performing artists of all kinds have traditionally perfected their skills before mirrors; micro-teaching allows student teachers to examine themselves in the third person and review how they operate in the classroom; videotapes are used in training industrial operators; and computer-based management games often contain a record of how the game was played, so that participants can become more aware of what they are doing.

What have all these situations in common? The answer is that, in each case, the learner has access to a behavioural record — a sort of reflected image — on which to base future improvement. The idea in each situation is the same: if people are aware of what they are presently doing, and can be encouraged to reflect on it and to consider alternatives, they are in an excellent position to change and to try out new ways of behaving.

These situations also have in common another, more subtle similarity for, in each case, the learner is independent. Instead of requiring an 'outsider' to provide the needed feedback about performance, the learner is able to observe, experiment, practise, and improve without the intervention of another. This is not to say that all skills are capable of infinite improvement without outside input or expert help, but rather that the responsibility for the learning process is put where it belongs — with the learner.

This, in fact, is consistent with most people's experience. By far the largest proportion of learning occurs in situations, without a teacher, which are neither planned nor mediated as educational, and in writing about the differences between formal, non-formal and informal education, Kleis notes:

> the day to day direct and unexamined experiences of living constitute the bases of beliefs, habits, values, attitudes, speech patterns and other character- istics of a person or people. Such experiences are educationally unintentional; but they are nonetheless powerful. The results are so common and they are produced so completely without awareness or intent that they are commonly thought to be 'natural' or 'inherent'. The fact is, of course, that they are learned. (Kleis, 1974, p6)

Clearly, the operative words in this quote are 'unexamined', 'awareness', and 'intent'. If people's awareness of what is happening to them can be heightened, and if they can intentionally examine life events, then they can make more of each experience. This is equally true of entering a new job, relating to a marriage partner, living on one's own, reading a book, making contributions to a postgraduate seminar, attending a lecture, or participating in an encounter group.

In recent years, many people who help others to learn — teachers, coaches, trainers and therapists — have seen the potential of reflective learning in helping learners to 'see themselves as others see them' and, in the process, to contemplate (or reflect on) what they see. Ironically, there is one major class of activities which, despite their central importance to us, have been relatively untouched by the notion of reflective learning: these are the skills of learning themselves.

Most students are almost totally unaware of how they attribute meaning to the things they encounter in lectures, laboratories, libraries, seminars, work placements and elsewhere. Reading, listening, talking, writing, thinking, feeling, judging, deciding and doing are, for most of us, long established habits which have become so fixed and unavailable to conscious review, that the learner is almost entirely a prisoner of his or her rigid competencies. Recognizing this problem, the Centre for the Study of Human Learning at Brunel University has, since 1968, been developing a model of 'learning to learn' using a range of approaches which help people to become reflective self-organized learners.

It is not easy to videotape learning, and to play it back for later analysis. In fact, learning is a rather elusive activity, which cannot be directly observed at all. Thus the Centre has concentrated on developing a range of techniques and devices which enables learners to explore, review and develop the ways in which they learn from books, lectures, seminars, problem-solving situations, project work, laboratory investigations, as well as 'on the job', in the factory, hospital or boardroom.

Despite certain superficial similarities, however, this approach is not to be confused with the recent upsurge of interest in conducting study skills programmes — many of which are designed to encourage the skills of taking 'good' notes, writing 'correct' exam scripts, or contributing 'appropriately' as a member of a tutorial group. Such so called 'learning to learn' programmes are really no more than courses on 'learning to submit to being taught', and they leave the students totally dependent on the content and structure of the formal course of study, without increasing their ability to learn independently or 'pro-actively' (Knowles, 1975).

The remainder of this chapter is devoted to a discussion of some of the reflective learning devices which have been developed at the Centre, but first, it is essential to introduce the concept of a learning conversation.

Learning Conversations

When we think of reflective learning, we usually have in mind a solitary kind of activity, in which the learner contemplates or reviews some insight or experience in order to reach new understandings. But reflection does not always start off this way; very often it begins with someone talking over his or her ideas with another person, and using them as a 'sounding board' — in everyday language we talk about 'thinking out loud'.

This simple idea gave rise to the notion of a learning conversation, a form of dialogue about a learning experience in which the learner reflects on some event or activity in the past. Ultimately, it is intended that people will internalize such conversations so that they are able to review learning experiences systematically for themselves, but at the beginning, the learning conversation is carried out with the assistance of a teacher or tutor.

It must first of all be said that a learning conversation is not idle chatter, nor is it an exchange of prescriptions, instructions or injunctions. Instead, it is a dialogue on the process of learning: the learner reflects on his or her learning with the assistance of a teacher or tutor. The quality or nature of this dialogue, however, shifts as the learning conversation progresses.

There has been a good deal of research on retraining, and a recurrent finding is that long established patterns of behaviour are remarkably persistent and difficult to change. Whether it is kicking a football, driving a car, reading a book, operating a piece of industrial equipment, or indeed almost any other skill, something which has become habitual has a remarkably self-sustaining capacity. When people first set out to improve their performance through reflective learning, they notice a distinct drop-off in performance once their habitual level of skill is disrupted. This phenomenon is sometimes referred to as conscious incompetence. Take, for instance, the case of a teacher who is asked to develop an awareness of himself or herself as a teacher. In this case, attention is divided between observing, and the behaviour being observed, with the likelihood of a decrease in teaching competence. Not unnaturally, there is a tendency to want to re-establish equilibrium at the old level, which can be depicted diagrammatically as follows:

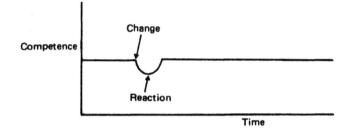

Recognizing this, it is the responsibility of the teacher, trainer or therapist to support and encourage the learner through such a depression, and then to help the learner to restabilize at a new, higher level of performance.

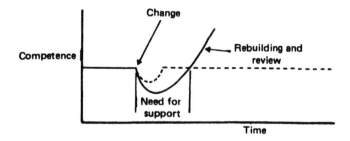

There is another curious feature about the maintenance of stable habits, and that is that even improved performance has a tendency to drop off, or return to old levels, unless new skills become internalized, and the learner becomes comfortable at the new, higher levels of operation. This can be shown like this:

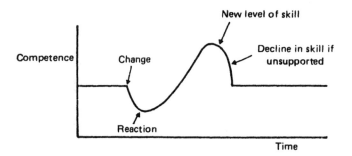

Thus, if the tutor or trainer is trying to help the learner to maintain improved standards of performance, it is necessary to identify the new criteria for the higher level of competence, and to support the learner until that new behaviour or level of skill has become habitual.

The effect of all this is to indicate the need for different types of dialogue at different points along the learning curve. First, there is the intervention point, the 'mirroring' or feedback which needs to be specific, behavioural and non-interpretative. Then the trainer has to deal with the emotional context of the learning, building up a supportive relationship which helps the learner through the period of trauma and disintegration of skills. Finally, the teacher or trainer helps the learner to articulate the new dimensions of quality. The learner needs to identify referents with which he or she can identify — significant others, peers or professional groups; this must provide the learner with new standards against which to measure performance, but without generating into a dogmatic system of rules.

An example may help to make the point. Imagine that you are helping people to improve their performance as drivers. For most adults, driving a car is an overlearned skill, one which we perform routinely and without much conscious thought. Unfortunately this extends to bad driving habits as well as good ones, and it may be that you seek to help some people to eradicate some aspect of their driving which is undesirable. As soon as you ask them to consider consciously what they are doing (changing gears, braking, accelerating, steering etc) the chances are that they will become confused and self-conscious, and that their fluency or facility as drivers will suffer accordingly. This is the decrease in skill level to which we have already referred.

If you manage to support them through this phase, and to bring about the desired change in driving skills, the next problem you will face is the likelihood of their 'backsliding' or slipping back into old habits and patterns as soon as they stop concentrating. It is at this stage that you will need to provide new referents, or new ways of judging themselves, until new habitual patterns are established. This, of course, is the age-old problem of unlearning and retraining which researchers such as those at the Industrial Training Research Unit in Cambridge have been grappling with for years, but it is considerably more complex if the learner is not only trying to master the new skill, but also to monitor and reflect on the process of mastering the new skill at the same time. In the final analysis, it is the intention for learners not only to be able to reflect on their own performance, but then to carry that reflection through systematically to a new, enhanced level of performance, on their own.

From this general discussion of learning conversations, we move on to a consideration of some of the tools or devices which have been developed by the Centre for the Study of Human Learning to promote reflective learning *about* learning processes.

The Brunel Reading Recorder

One of the basic skills of learning is the ability to read, and most successful learners have at least several distinct reading strategies. Yet most people, when they read, are aware neither of how they read, nor of the cognitive and affective processes which underlie their behaviour. To the extent that they are unaware, reading becomes a marionette-like mechanical activity. Even if they try to develop awareness, enormous difficulties are experienced in observing their reading-for-learning processes. One outstanding experience is that they are unable to remember themselves reading. This is the situation from which they must start learning-to-learn about their reading. Only by guiding learners back into contact with their own process can they become aware of the existing state of their skills and bring these under review.

The reading recorder has been developed as a way of recording how much time is spent as a learner reads a text, showing changes in pace, hesitations, skipping forwards or backwards and taking notes (Thomas and Harri-Augstein, 1973). An example of a read record obtained from the reading recorder appears as Figure 1.

However, it is not enough simply to record, and then to 'play back' how a learner read something. It is necessary to go back over the reading, reconstructing what the learner was doing at each phase and (perhaps more important) why. It is only when the learners begin to become aware of their own processes of reading, that the possibility exists to monitor and ultimately to change their strategy at will. Thus, it is the responsibility of the 'teacher' to go through the read record with the learners offering possible interpretations and helping them to acquire the skills of interpreting for themselves.

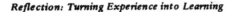
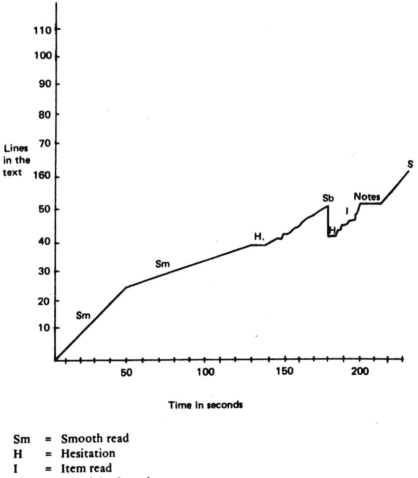

Sm = Smooth read
H   = Hesitation
I   = Item read
Sb = Search backwards
Note: This read record is simplified for clarity

Figure 1 *A read record obtained on the reading recorder*

This may appear trivial, but the quality of the learning conversation depends on this sensitivity to the information on the record. The verbal ability to talk about a read record is not the same as the perceptual ability to recognize significant events in the process of reading from the pen-recording emitted by the machine. The teacher or teaching participant is not just aiming to *describe* what happened to the learner, but to help the learner to 'relive' the particular piece of reading. A typical review might go like this:

Tutor   '. . . You started at line 1 and read evenly through to line 23 where you began to slow down and read at about half your original speed until line 37. Here you stopped for 20 seconds . . . was this of any significance for you?'

Student 'I am not sure . . . Oh yes . . . I couldn't understand that phrase . . . and that term . . . really threw me . . . this bit on lines 37-38 I found really interesting, though I disagree with the author . . .'

Tutor   'How relevant was all this to your purpose?'

Student 'Well . . . perhaps I did get a bit bogged down with the text and I shouldn't really have spent time on evaluating these ideas . . . after all, I did say I was aiming to get the gist . . . an overview.'

Tutor   'So?'

Student 'Maybe I ought to bear in mind that I shouldn't let the author take me over if I'm to get a quick overview . . . my record should be much smoother . . . fewer hesitations . . . no notes.'

Tutor   'Now on lines 40-49 you skipped backwards, hesitated, read on and made some notes. What was the point of this?'

Student 'I wanted to recall the details exactly and I wanted to check it later.'

Tutor   'What kind of notes did you make?'

Student 'They were pretty detailed, almost a copy of the text.'

Tutor   'Is this your usual way of making notes?'

Student 'Yes, on the whole. I know it wasn't really necessary here to try to remember these details, but I was worried that if I didn't I might not really understand the text.'

Tutor   'We might get you to explore this in depth next time.'

Further discussion encourages the learners to explore exactly why they read the text in that particular way. This form of organized talk-back through a read record encourages the learner to explore exactly why he or she read the text in a particular way, to identify key habits, and to explore and develop new strategies; what this review does not do, however, is to permit the reader to reconstruct and display the meaning within a text.

The Flow Diagram Technique

The linear nature of a text leads us into believing that the meaning is also uniform and linear; however, within any given piece of reading, there are likely to be main themes, qualifications and elaborations, and linking items — joining one part to another. Because people construct meaning differently (ie no two people are likely to read a piece of text and gain precisely the same understanding from it), it is useful for learners to reflect on how they unravel a text and attribute personally relevant meaning to it.

Having created an awareness of the process of reading by talk-back through the read record, the flow diagram technique is introduced in the learning conversation. This technique permits the reader to display the meaning within the text. Figure 2 shows how specific categories and items of text are displayed so that the original linear sequence is preserved but the structure of the text is unravelled.

This flow diagram technique can be utilized at any level in the organization of a reading task. The reading of single sentences can be recorded, and a multi-dimensional description of the phrases which make up items of meaning in the sentence can be displayed. Likewise, it is possible to obtain a flow diagram of all the sentences in a paragraph, paragraphs in a chapter, or chapters in a book.

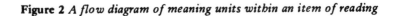

Figure 2 *A flow diagram of meaning units within an item of reading*

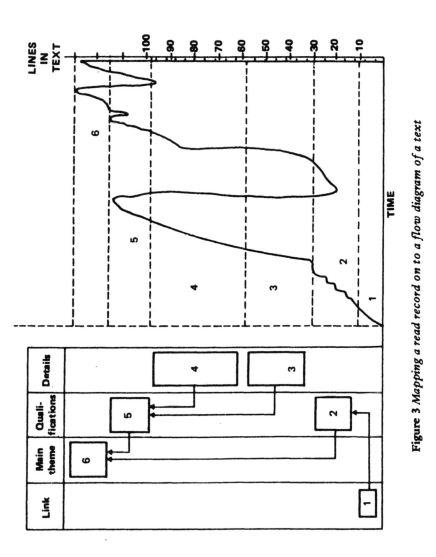

Figure 3 *Mapping a read record on to a flow diagram of a text*

This sort of intensive analysis might seem somewhat laboured and even irrelevant, but once we have a detailed picture of how the learners are interpreting a text by constructing a personally relevant flow diagram, it is possible to superimpose this on to their read record to obtain a reconstruction and evaluation of their reading-for-learning process. In other words, the learners can be made aware, perhaps for the first time, of the way in which meaning is attributed as they slow down, hesitate, take notes or skip backwards and forwards through the text.

Once a learner has produced a read record and a flow diagram for the same piece of text, together the tutor and the learner can interpret the record and flow diagram by relating these to the original text and to the learner's purpose for reading. It is, of course, essential for the tutor to develop sensitivity in the talk-back process and to empathize with the readers. For many people, going through such an intensive breakdown of a small reading task can be frustrating, and this can lead to stress in the conversational encounter. Often, learners will make comments like, 'I'm going on with this all day, even if it kills me', 'I will never get this right', 'I'm beginning to hate flow diagrams', or 'Psychologists who meddle in other people's learning should have their own heads read!' What is needed at times like this is a caring attitude — the sort of support dialogue discussed above.

An experienced trainer will soon develop a feeling for whether the learners are actually reliving the reading experience, or simply going through the motions of reproducing their thought patterns and feelings. Talking a person back into the reading-for-learning experience is an important component of the awareness-raising technique. While there is obviously no objective check on the validity of the re-creation of the experiential process, there are numerous corroborative indicators. Spontaneous remarks which relate to the content of the text and to the monitoring and decision-making processes, together with the readers' apparent recognition of their earlier experience, all add up. Part of the skill in conducting a learning conversation is to be able to talk readers back into their earlier process with some evaluative commentary attached, so that they are able to review the process of learning.

The Structure of Meaning Technique

Linked to the flow diagram technique is another device which helps a learner to reflect on how he or she is actually structuring new knowledge. This is the structure of meaning technique (Thomas and Harri-Augstein, 1976), which allows learners to display in a diagrammatic way, what they see as important items of meaning and how these are related to one another. This technique, while it can be used in almost any type of learning, is particularly relevant to the skills of listening. In his book on thinking, *Use Your Head*, Buzan (1978) comments that the linear nature of speech has obscured the complex process of sorting and selecting which is going on both in speaking and in listening:

. . . the listener is not simply observing a long list of words like someone sucking up spaghetti. He is receiving each word in the context of the words that surround it. At the same time he is also giving the multi-ordinate nature of each word his own special interpretation as dictated by the structure of his personal information patterns and will be analysing, coding and criticising throughout the process . . .

If the brain is to relate to information most efficiently the information must be structured in such a way as to 'slot in' as easily as possible. It follows that if the brain works primarily with key concepts in an interlinked and integrated manner, our notes and our word relations should in many instances be structured in this way rather than in traditional 'lines'.

Rather than starting from the top and working down in sentences or lists, one should start from the centre or main idea and branch out as dictated by the individual ideas and general form of the central theme. (Buzan, 1978, pp86-88)

Thus, with the structure of meaning technique, the learner, listener or reader attempts to illustrate by diagrammatic means the main areas of any field, and their interrelationships. A highly simplified structure of meaning is shown in Figure 4.

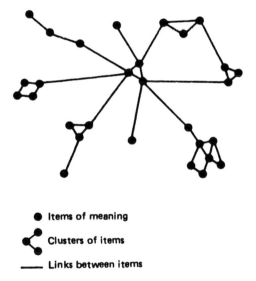

● Items of meaning

◀ Clusters of items

▬▬ Links between items

Figure 4 *A structure of meaning*

As in the reading example, talking back through this structure of meaning can raise awareness of how learners are structuring their own learning. It also allows learners to share their experiences. Comparing meaning attributed to the same event, eg a lecture or a book, is an important aspect of the learning conversation. Patterns A and B in Figure 5 show two 'structures of meaning' attributed by two learners to the same event. If they try to share and explain their individual perspectives to each other, each becomes more aware of alternative patterns of understanding, thus extending their own experience and generating richer structures of meaning of a given event.

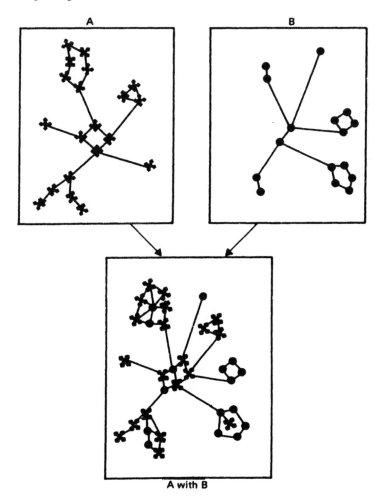

Figure 5 *Sharing two structures of meaning*

The Repertory Grid

Bearing in mind that the ultimate aim of all learning-to-learn activities is to develop 'self-organized' learners who are capable of monitoring and reflecting on their own learning processes, probably one of the most promising techniques developed by the Centre is the repertory grid technique. This is an outgrowth of Kelly's *Psychology of Personal Constructs* (1955), and it is essentially a way of recording in their own words how people understand some part of their world.

The grid is a vehicle for exploring the experiential world (thoughts and feelings) of an individual. The grid elicitation interview consists of two phases. In the first phase, the participant is asked to name a range of 'elements' which would define a 'universe of discourse'. For instance, you could choose to explore your ideas about effective and ineffective management, and some of the elements might be, 'the most effective manager I ever knew', 'the least effective manager I ever knew', 'my present boss', 'myself as a manager', 'my former boss' and 'three other managers in my organization'.

When a representative sample of elements has been elicited, the subject is then moved into the second phase of the interview. This is concerned with eliciting 'constructs' and assigning elements to the poles of these constructs. Specifically, each element is written on a card and the subject is offered three cards at a time. He or she is asked to think about the three elements and to decide which two out of the three are most alike. Again, sensitive interviewing can enhance the quality of the response. When a similar pair has been identified the subject is asked to describe the nature of the similarity. This description constitutes one pole of the construct. A description of how the third card or singleton differs from the pair is then elicited. This constitutes the second pole of the construct.

To take our earlier example, you might be presented with the three cards 'most effective manager', 'present boss' and 'last boss'. In looking at these, you might respond that 'most effective manager' and 'last boss' are alike because they were both good communicators, and this would then become one pole of your construct. The third person is different because he does not communicate well, and so 'poor communicator' might be the opposite end of that construct.

Once these poles have been elicited the subject is then asked to rank or rate all the individual elements along that construct dimension. This procedure is repeated a number of times, using fresh sets of three elements each time, until the respondent's repertoire of constructs is exhausted.

Thus, the repertory grid technique makes explicit respondents' views of significant elements in their thinking and feeling about a topic and the dimensions in which the topic is thought about. Constructing this raw grid is a useful reflective exercise in itself; the subjects become immediately more aware of the topic and of the framework in which they perceive it. However the grid can be subjected to various forms of analysis and internal reorganization which makes it even more powerful as an awareness-raising tool for reflective learning.

Although the technique was originally developed as a paper and pencil device to be used by a therapist and a client in a conversational setting, one of the major advances of the Centre for the Study of Human Learning has been to make the grid elicitation process available through the use of a computer. In this context, the learner sits down and is 'interrogated' in a friendly way by a computer, and the responses form the elements, constructs and matrix which make up the grid. While the computer potentially suffers, at least at first, from the dual threats of impersonality and loss of privacy, once users have overcome their apprehension, they are uniquely placed to engage in challenging and rewarding forms of reflective learning, by systematically reflecting on their own personal world views.

Other Tools to Aid Reflective Learning

In recent years, the Centre has further extended the boundaries of reflective learning. Using the two major ingredients — namely the speed and capacity of the computer and the compelling power of learning through a behavioural record — the Centre has developed a unique range of reflective learning tools. These include computer-driven videos, computer-simulated radar screens and all manner of variations built around the basic theme of the repertory grid. In all cases, these devices have the following characteristics:

1. Some observational record or external display of one aspect of learning. Purpose-strategy-outcome-review can each be separately and integratively investigated by means of awareness-raising tools.
2. A display of the learning process which facilitates effective talk-back, so that the learning event can be re-experienced.
3. A capacity to look at the skill at a very general or a very detailed level, or anywhere in between, so that learners can continue to develop their learning-to-learn at different levels of complexity.
4. Not only new ways of looking at skills, but new ways of describing them, both to themselves and to other people, so that the description of behaviour and experience can be in sufficient detail and with such a degree of precision that a new level of awareness is achieved.
5. A procedure for gradually weaning away from dependency on the tools, replacing these with an enhanced perception and language through which the learner can achieve the same effect unsupported from the outside.

Summary and Conclusion

It has been the purpose of this chapter to explore just one example of reflection in learning — namely reflection in learning how to learn — for we agree with Rogers (1969) when he writes:

> The most socially useful learning in the modern world is the learning of the process of learning: a continuing openness to experience and incorporation into oneself of the process of change. (Rogers, 1969)

Our experience leads us to believe that much potentially valuable learning is 'lost' because learners have not developed the skills of recreating or reliving learning episodes which they experience. For most people, their responses to learning events tend to be habitual and unquestioned, and practice (even repeated practice) does not allow them to make explicit the connection between what Argyris and Schon (1974) call their 'theory in use' and their actions. What is required, it seems to us, is the opportunity for learners to reflect on their performance, but reflection is not facilitated simply by allowing time for it, or even by offering questions to encourage thinking and critical self-awareness. No, in the first instance, reflection is facilitated by providing some sort of behavioural record (such as a videotape, an observation sheet or a computer analysis) of the learner in the learning situation.

The next step is to take learners through this behavioural record conversationally — prompting here, probing there, inquiring somewhere else, but all the time encouraging the learners to relive the experience and to express in their own words why they behaved the way they did. Once they have brought to a level of conscious awareness the strategies and values which were previously implicit, they are in a position to modify them and then to try them out again in another situation.

Our work has shown that as people reflect on themselves and on their performance in some setting, they open themselves up to the possibility of change. As Rogers (1969) observes:

> Learning which involves a change in self organisation — in the perception of oneself — is threatening and tends to be resisted. (Rogers, 1969)

Hence, the process of reflection carries with it some threat, and it thus needs to be handled sensitively by whoever is managing the learning situation; we call this the support dialogue.

Finally, we argue that the aim of reflective learning is to develop learners who are capable of monitoring themselves in a variety of situations. In other words, it should be the intention of the teacher or trainer ultimately to make himself or herself redundant, and to develop in the learners the ability to reflect on their own processes as learners.

Conversational methodology promises to be an effective alternative to pre-planned teaching programmes for promoting self-organized learning. It offers procedures for enhancing awareness and the development of processes (Thomas and Harri-Augstein, 1977). The tools and procedures for conducting 'learning conversations' are seen as temporary devices which participants can recruit and discard as they develop their competency; indeed there is nothing to stop people from inventing new tools and techniques if they want to work on some particular aspect of their learning-to-learn skills. Prospective interactions with each other and with resources, which may take the form of *ad hoc* chats, formal lectures, informal forums, will be enriched by the newly gained skills for giving personal relevance to these learning experiences. Self-organized participants can judge when to turn to others for support and guidance. The beginnings of a science of learning conversations backed by theory and specialist tools now exist (Polanyi, 1967; Pask, 1976; Thomas, 1978); the arena is wide open for educational psychologists to build on this in their own individual ways.

References

Argyris, C and Schon, D A (1974) *Theory in Practice: Increasing Professional Effectiveness*, San Francisco: Jossey-Bass

Buzan, T (1978) *Use Your Head*, London: BBC Publications

Kelly, G A (1955) *The Psychology of Personal Constructs*, Vols I and II, New York: Norton

Kleis, R (1974) *Case Studies in Non-Formal Education*, Institute for International Studies in Education, East Lansing: Michigan State University

Knowles, M (1975) *Self Directed Learning: A Guide for Learners and Teachers*, New York: Association Press

Pask, G (1976) Conversational techniques in the study and practice of education, *British Journal of Educational Psychology*, Vol 46, pp12-25

Polanyi, M (1967) *The Tacit Dimension*, New York: Doubleday

Rogers, C R (1969) *Freedom-to-Learn: A View of What Education might Become*, Columbus, Ohio: Merrill

Thomas, L F (1973) 'The Flow Diagram Technique' Paper. Centre for the Study of Human Learning, Brunel University

Thomas, L F (1978) A personal construct approach to learning in education, training and therapy, in Fransella, F (ed) (1977) *Personal Construct Psychology*, London: Academic Press

Thomas, L F and Harri-Augstein, E S (1973) *Developing Your Own Reading*, Milton Keynes: Open University Press

Thomas, L F and Harri-Augstein, E S (1976) 'Structures of Meaning', Centre for the Study of Human Learning, Brunel University

Thomas, L F and Harri-Augstein, E S (1977) *The Art and Science of Getting a Degree*, Centre for the Study of Human Learning, Brunel University

CHAPTER 8
Judging the Quality of Development

Philip Boxer, *London Business School*

> Would any of you think of building a tower without first sitting down and calculating the cost, to see whether he could afford to finish it? Otherwise, if he has laid its foundation and then is not able to complete it, all the on-lookers will laugh at him. 'There is the man', they will say, 'who started to build and could not finish.' Or what king will march to battle against another king, without first sitting down to consider whether with ten thousand men he can face an enemy coming to meet him with twenty thousand? If he cannot, then, long before the enemy approaches, he sends envoys, and asks for terms. So also none of you can be a disciple of mine without parting with all his possessions. (Luke 14: 28-33) (Taken from the Jerusalem Bible, published and copyright 1966, 1967 and 1968 by Darton, Longman and Todd Ltd and Doubleday & Co Inc, and used by permission of the publishers.)

Introduction

Ten years ago, I embarked on the development of techniques for working with managers which could enable the manager to develop the quality of his judgement (Boxer, 1978). The focus of this work was on choices which were 'strategic' for the manager. In the beginning I defined 'strategic' in terms of the situation in which the manager found himself: he experienced some ambiguity in the nature of the problems he faced. In retrospect, I was concerned with enabling the manager to have a strategy. Over the years this concern has become inverted. Now I see it as one of enabling the manager to be strategic: defining 'strategic' in relation to the manager's self. Hence judging the quality of development is something for the manager to do and not me. This chapter seeks to follow the course of this inversion, and to consider where it leaves me. The whole view of development which unfolds in this chapter, however, speaks from these pages with a male voice. A female voice would speak of the end as my beginning. No matter, because 'development' seems to have been more of a male preoccupation to date, and perhaps there is something for us to learn here therefore. Anyway, I wrote the chapter backwards!

The origins of the project lay in my experience of management education, and the difficulties I had in balancing what I was learning in formal courses with what I was able to learn from my experience. Thanks to funding initially from the National Development Programme in Computer Assisted Learning (NDPCAL) (Hooper, 1977), and later from the Training Services Division of the UK Manpower Services Commission (Boot, 1979), methods of working with managers emerged which became known as reflective analysis (Shaw, 1981), and which were based on the repertory grid technique (Fransella and Bannister, 1977). Reflective analysis was intended to enable the manager to involve, engage with and develop his experience-based knowledge.

Teaching Paradigms

The evaluators of the NDPCAL project described reflective analysis as belonging within a 'conjectural' paradigm which could be distinguished from an 'instructional', 'revelatory' or 'emancipatory' paradigm. The teacher can do two things: he can frame problems through the point of view from which he examines them; and he can present particular ways of picturing what is seen through the ways in which he makes sense of what he sees. Using these two concepts of the 'frame' and the 'picture', we can distinguish between these paradigms in terms of whether or not the teacher provides the frame and/or the picture or allows them to be free for the learner to choose.

Within the instructional paradigm, the primary concern is in the learning of particular ways of making sense of particular problems — this paradigm best characterizes traditional classroom teaching in which the knowledge needed is specified and transmitted to the manager in such a way that both the picture and its frame are given. The revelatory paradigm presents a given picture within which certain things are known about a particular problem, but encourages the manager to develop his own point of view within which to make sense of what he sees, even though this freedom is limited by the nature of the picture. Case teaching and the use of simulations are characteristic of this paradigm because they permit freedom in how the manager interprets what is going on while presenting a particular reality. Finally the emancipatory paradigm provides the manager with a particular tool which can be applied to a range of problems but which carries with it assumptions about the point of view from which the problem can be examined. This tool may be a particular behavioural skill or a mathematical algorithm, but in being used, it evokes a particular way of framing the problem — it assumes a particular approach. These differences can be summarized in the diagram shown in Figure 1.

The conjectural paradigm differs from the other paradigms in that it seeks to leave the manager free both to choose how he makes sense of things, and also what he makes sense of. Reflective analysis as a technique is certainly content-free and open-ended in the ways in which it enables the manager to interpret his experience. As a technique, therefore, it demands that the teacher works within the conjectural paradigm, as he would have to with action research and action learning. Even though the teacher is required to be conjectural, however, it does not follow that the manager will be. In practice, the manager was never conjectural, but rather used reflective analysis in a revelatory way. The following comment, made by a manager following his experience of reflective analysis, was characteristic:

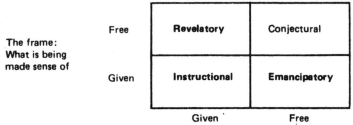

Figure 1 *Teaching paradigms*

> The main problem in describing our work together is one of labels. What happened was not a 'course', nor was it psychoanalysis. I suppose, if I have to attach a label to it, it was a process of increasing awareness of the emotional culture in which I operate; that culture being one of the most important limiting factors to my performance as an individual and, more important, as a member of a number of groups of people.

Working reflectively then enabled the manager to reframe his own experience as he had defined it to himself. Even to himself, however, his experience was 'given'. Thus reflective analysis became a process for enabling personal revelation. What then is involved in reflective analysis?

Working Reflectively

Reflective analysis is a technique through which the manager can examine the way in which he frames his experience. He can do this either by reflecting on the historical parallels to the present situation (past reflection), or by reflecting on the bases underlying the present choices open to him (option analysis). These two ways of reflecting move along the two axes of the manager's experience of the present moment: the diachronic axis through which the manager experiences the past as extending through the present into the future, and the synchronic axis whereby he renders the moment distinctly present. Either way he is framing his experience, although his historical determinism is more apparent in past reflection. The following example gives some feel for how one manager defined some of his past experience in relation to options he faced as to how he spent his time:

Past experiences	Present options
Uncle figure	Pricing issues
Moving	Directors' meetings
Chartered accountant	Strategy review
Scots	Chairman's meetings
John	Monthly staff briefing
Computer	Customer contact
Exam	Plant visits

There are no rules as to how the manager arrives at these lists. Producing these lists, however, involved him in distilling out of his past experience or present situation relevant detail which he wished to reflect upon. He was therefore starting the process from a particular frame. This was not always easy for him to do, but I shall return to the problems inherent in adopting this first position later. Having framed his experience by choosing particular experiences on which he wished to reflect, he then began to pattern the detail in terms of a number of concepts, thus building up a picture. The concepts are labels for particular ways in which he patterned the particular experiences, and some examples of concepts from the same manager follow:

Integrity	Nailed down
I've got to fight	Good for my future
Look at me	Not busy busy
Path finding	Clear focus
Piously hopeful	Developing long term
My feelings don't matter	Impact on problems
Dropping bricks	Love it

These concepts are describing the manager's sense of relatedness in his experience. The patterns are created by arranging letters representing each individual experience or option along a line. The manager actually rated 18 past experiences in terms of 'look at me', each one of which was given a key letter. Seven of these past experiences were listed above and are represented by the letters A/C/G/J/N/O/R (but not in this order) in the following pattern:

Low   **High**

J--- C-- PDI--QB----O---A--R--- FK--- H--LE---M---G---N

Look at me

Thus the past experience represented by the letter 'N' is experienced by this manager as exemplifying a very high degree of 'look at me', 'J' as a very low degree, and 'O', 'A' and 'R' as being relatively indifferent. The detail of the method is described in Boxer (1981b), but in essence it is very simple: it uses as a basis for reflection an analysis of the similarities in the patterns, which can be expressed in terms either of the concepts or of the experiences or options. In the analysis of the concepts based on the past reflection above, part of the 'tree' of concepts came out as shown on page 121.

The important part of the reflective process comes from giving meaning to these similarities and differences. What seems to happen is that the manager's ideas of what sense there ought to be in his experience, as implicit in the original position which he has taken, is challenged by the sense which emerges out of the patterns which he has described in his experience. In this 'tree' of concepts, the manager was asking 'Why, when I am saying "Look at me" to myself, am I also usually saying "Let me out" . . .?' On reflection, his answer was another

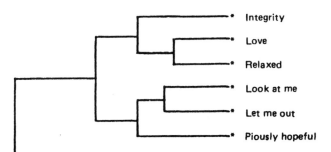

- Integrity
- Love
- Relaxed
- Look at me
- Let me out
- Piously hopeful

concept which embraced a larger patterning of experience which could then be set alongside 'piously hopeful'. This process continued until the manager had reduced his concepts to a smaller number, each one of which embraced a particular voice through which his experiences spoke to him. By becoming aware of them, he is thereby able to interrogate them. That is reflective analysis — recognizing the voices through which his experience speaks to him. The following comment by a different manager conveys something of the result:

> Getting to know myself through important events and activities was fascinating. Self-analysis by computer? The idea is ridiculous, the concept intriguing, the practice quite practical. The objective viewpoint given me by the computer printout distanced me enough to allow me to see my activities in a new light. The juxtaposition of perhaps less likely events forced me to really analyse what happened in those events, and how I learned from them . . . trying to open new approaches to my experiences was a stimulating experience for me. (An MSc student's comment on the use of the technique on a course entitled 'Learning as a subversive activity', Boxer, 1981a)

This technique then enables the manager to examine the ways in which he frames his own experiences: the ways in which he is able to give meanings to them. Reflective analysis leads him to be aware that his experiences speak to him through more than one voice. This presents the manager with a new issue: on what basis is he to choose how to frame his experience? In learning to ask himself this question, the manager is learning to be critical of his own development, but by what authority? Here is a quotation from an evaluation of a workshop which made extensive use of the reflective method:

> By the end of the Workshop, the participants talked freely amongst themselves and to me about experiencing 'breakthrough'. This breakthrough was particularly associated with working reflectively. What seemed to be happening was that the reflective method had enabled them to 'know' in a conscious sense what and how they were experiencing both within and outside the Workshop. This 'knowledge' was enabling them to manage their own learning in qualitatively different ways. NIPPER* as an analytical technique was an essential part of this process, not because it was doing something which could not otherwise be done, but rather because it enabled the individual's reflection to sustain a very high degree of focus on the quality of his own experience. (Boot and Boxer, 1980, p250)

*NIPPER is the name of the software for supporting reflective analysis developed by the project referred to in the introduction. It is presently available from the author as 'micro-NIPPER' for implementation on CP/M microcomputers.

The outcome of this process was sometimes totally inconsequential, and sometimes dramatic for the manager: he changed his job, or adopted a radically new way of acting in his life. On occasions, however, it led to a very high degree of anxiety, as the questions it raised heightened the tension between what the 'voices' suggested were true, and what the manager thought ought to be true. This anxiety was associated with his experiencing an absence of authority from which to choose. In these circumstances, the manager seemed to be stuck, putting considerable energy into avoiding working reflectively. As a result, he was unwilling to be critical of, or get leverage on, his development. It was in trying to find ways of responding creatively to this 'stuckness' that my understanding of the nature of 'strategic' became inverted. There was much to be learnt, however, from the ways in which the manager avoided choosing.

Strategies for Avoiding Choosing

Over the years I had developed a sense of there being three distinct ways in which managers became stuck: their stuckness manifested itself as fragmentation, alienation or impotence. Fragmentation was a kind of all-consuming 'busyness' in which the manager seemed to have vast numbers of things to get done by yesterday, with none of them leading anywhere. Alienation took the form of having lots of things to be done with good reason for doing every one of them, but with no feeling that any of them mattered at all. Finally the impotent manager was unable to connect events as they were unfolding with his desires for the form which he felt they should be taking.

Each of these forms of stuckness had severe implications for the business if the manager who was stuck also had some responsibility for developing the business. His fragmentation led to incoherence in what he was doing, and an inability to sustain the initiatives he took; alienation meant that he never really seemed able to develop anything at all, despite making himself enormously busy; and impotence meant that despite all his power, he could never really find ways of using it which seemed to have any significant effect. In each case the manager could say 'I have tried everything that I can think of, and still nothing works.' Under these circumstances, what would be more natural than to seek out an expert who could provide a ready-made solution?

The original project (Hooper, 1977) set out with the aim of developing teaching methods to be used by teachers to enhance the manager's awareness of the concepts he used in decision-making situations, and to help the manager in developing those concepts to evolve new ones. Computer-based simulations of various industries and case studies were used to provide contexts for training experiences. Why was it necessary to use simulations and case studies as context? Surely managers had enough 'context' of their own — why create yet more contexts for them? The simulations were very successful as such, and made it possible for large numbers of managers to develop their skills and resourcefulness.

But always there was the problem of defining relevance and transferring learning back into the managers' 'real' worlds.

It is true that many of the difficulties I encountered in developing the use of reflective analysis were associated with persuading teachers to set up learning experiences within the conjectural paradigm, so that managers could learn in ways which they could make relevant and timely to their concerns. The major proportion of my time in the early years was taken up with finding ways of dealing with this problem by trying to challenge the ways in which teachers and trainers chose to frame learning experiences. The easy explanation for these difficulties was that it was comfortable for teachers to work in the revelatory, instructional or emancipatory paradigms, because it meant that they had something to give, and therefore provided them with a basis for their careers. This was true, but not the whole explanation, because it was the managers who were choosing to come on the courses.

Let us assume that at some level the manager knew that choosing to work reflectively with his own reality would lead him to having to face up to taking or not taking responsibility for creating his own solutions. How much easier it would be for him to opt for adopting someone else's solutions instead, thus postponing the choice and, at the same time, retaining control of what the experience meant for him as a result of the transfer problems created in trying to adopt the teacher's ready-made solution.

The conclusion I reached was that the ways in which managers became stuck were no more than the result of their having abdicated their own sense of authority in favour of the teacher's, and accepting the teacher's 'givens' without question. Each form of stuckness therefore could be understood in terms of the inappropriate adoption of a particular teaching paradigm: the revelatory paradigm meant taking the way in which sense was made of things as given so that impotence followed because nothing could be done differently. The emancipatory paradigm meant taking as given what could be made sense of so that the manager was always holding bits from someone else's picture which he could therefore never fit together within his own frame. Finally the instructional paradigm meant taking everything as given, so that the manager never even started considering what he should be working with for himself. Accepting fragmentation, alienation or impotence was the price paid in each case for not questioning the taken-as-given bases of meaning.

So even though the teachers could genuinely help some of the managers some of the time, more often than not they could not help. That did not really matter, however, because the manager was mostly not there to learn but to avoid learning by adopting the teacher's solutions rather than applying himself to developing his own. The characteristic of the manager who did not get caught up in this collusion was that he was not seeking to have a strategy: he was able to be strategic because he had a sense of his own authority. The inversion between 'having a strategy' and 'being strategic' began to take its course, therefore, when I realized that the

The frame:
What is being
made sense of

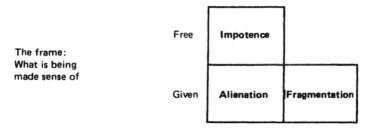

Given   Free
The picture: the way in which sense is made

Figure 2 *The consequences of copying teacher slavishly*

strategic thing for me to do was to work with these strategic managers.
I simply gave up trying to work from within an institutional and/or
company course teaching context, and began to work directly with the
manager within timeframes of his own choosing and with the issues that
surfaced for him out of his own context: I became self-employed.

By removing the institutional or training context, I was able to work
directly with the manager's reality within his organizational context.
Through engaging in a reflective process he was able to reframe his
experience in ways which felt true to his experience but which were
nevertheless surprising to him — he had not thought of looking at it like
that before. Where this was successful, this created a new kind of problem
for the manager. Although he was still dealing with his own reality, it was
no longer framed in a way which others could recognize: he had placed
himself within a different frame from that which had currency within his
organization. Thus although the outcomes of the process were valued by
him as a learning experience, because I had been working within the
conjectural paradigm, he could not explain his reframing by what I had
brought to the process. As a result he found himself in the position of
not having any way of describing its value as a distinct form of learning
experience to others; and the more deeply he had worked reflectively,
the less able he was to explain what he had been doing. He was thus
left with having to justify his working reflectively purely on the basis
of its value to himself, and the extent to which it enabled him to act
more strategically.

Two kinds of consequence seemed to flow, therefore, from working
reflectively: either it resulted in the manager experiencing an absence of
authority within himself from which to choose, in which case he was
brought face to face again with his own stuckness, but with a heightened
sense of anxiety; or it increased his sense of what he needed to do, but
left him less able to explain this to others.

The Self-employed Employee

What makes the manager choose to be strategic? Certainly it is this quality which enables the manager to take a position at the start of the reflective process. Yet the hardest part of all seems to be taking a position at the beginning. It is hard because in taking a position, the manager is choosing to apply critical consciousness to his own actions. Such a choice is the beginning of a one-way track for him along which nothing can be taken as given any more, not even the way in which his own consciousness presents reality to him. It is true that the teacher can seek to be as conjectural as possible in the way in which he relates to the manager, but if the manager does not take a position for himself, then nothing can be done.

The ability to take a position then is prior to engaging in any kind of reflective process which, as I gained experience of working with managers over longer periods of time, I began to see within the context of a longer term development process. This prior process I refer to as 'gathering'. In the process of gathering, the manager is learning to know for himself 'where he is at', 'where he is coming from', 'what is going on' and beginning to 'see things as they are'. The gathered manager is well able to provide the lists of concepts, options, experiences and so on which provide the starting point for reflective analysis. To be gathered, however, the manager has to learn to span a very complex reality. As I developed ways of working with the manager in this gathering process, I began to refer to the techniques I was using as 'projective analysis' because it became apparent to me that the nature of the picture which the manager formed for himself was a projection of the way in which he framed his experience. Thus to choose to take a position was to choose to know both what made sense to him and also the way in which it made sense to him. In Figure 3 he was moving into the bottom left position in relation to his experience, for while still knowing his identity in terms of his experience — being *of* his experience — he was distancing himself from his experience — *not in* his experience.

From this position of being *of* his experience but *not in* his experience, the reflective process could now be seen as one through which the manager could challenge the frame within which he knew himself. As I described earlier, this meant that the manager either fell back into being even more stuck, albeit knowing that he was stuck, or of accepting responsibility for his own authority in how he framed his experience — becoming self-employed. This process of reframing his experience I refer to as 'deconstruction'. Deconstruction involves the manager in questioning the relationship between the picture he sees and the way in which he frames it. When working with his own experience, therefore, this means questioning himself as a frame. Reflective analysis was therefore just one particular way in which the manager could question himself in this way, but as a process it was always difficult for the manager and demanded a great deal of commitment and persistence from him, most of all because it involved him in asking himself questions to which he did not already know the answers.

125

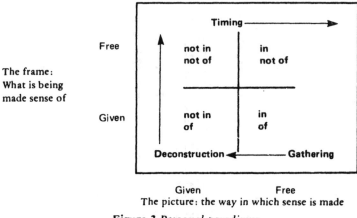

Figure 3 *Personal paradigms*

Gathering then brought the manager face to face with his identity as he knew it in terms of the world, and deconstruction brought him face to face with the horizons of his identity and led him to question its origins in himself. How then was this new-found sense of himself to become real in his actions and experience? Perhaps it could not ever be real. The manager was in a position of being *not in* and *not of* which could best be described as psychotic, since he was risking being unable to connect his sense of himself with his world. Not an easy place to be, and in stark contrast to the neurotic position of being *in* and *of* to which some managers returned with even greater stuckness.

The final stage of moving back into the world from a sense of himself which did not have its origins in the world — *in* and *not of* — was the stage which most distinguished the quality of being strategic, although of course all of the processes were bound up in being strategic. The main characteristic of this stage was a very great sensitivity to matters of timing. This involved having an ability to be very aware of the ways in which it was possible to connect himself with his actions and experience and a great sensitivity to the consequences both for himself and for others of those actions, with an acceptance, however, of the necessity to choose to act. Thus he was a self-employed employee in the sense that he had to accept the consequences of his actions, in relation to himself as well as to others.

By What Authority . . .

For the manager to be able to judge the quality of his own development he had to be prepared to take responsibility for being critical of his own development. This led him inexorably to having to choose. This, when all else has been said and done, became a matter of timing:

> There is timing in everything. Timing in strategy cannot be mastered without a great deal of practice . . . From the outset you must know the applicable timing and the inapplicable timing, and from among the large and small things and the fast and slow timings find the relevant timing, first seeing the distance timing and the background timing. This is the main thing in strategy. It is especially important to know the background timing, otherwise your strategy will become uncertain. (Musashi, 1645)

Even though it might not have been conscious, even the choice to start taking a position for himself in the first place was a matter of timing. In the end therefore, even though I had extended the range of managers and circumstances in relation to which I could work, the thing that I had begun to learn to do was to accept the timing as it presented itself, and never to assume that I could dictate it. The difficulty I had in doing this was in learning how to pay attention to timing without seeking to undermine it.

Postscript

Having finished this chapter, I find myself able to name the fourth form of stuckness: insignificance. It characterizes the experience of not being able to accept timing as it presents itself, and follows from being slavish about not copying teacher slavishly — conjecturalism for the sake of it.

References

Boot, R L (1979) The management learning project, *Industrial and Commercial Training*, Vol 11, No 1

Boot, R L and Boxer, P J (1980) Reflective learning, in Beck, J and Cox, C (eds) *Advances in Management Education*, Wiley

Boxer, P J (1978) Developing the quality of judgement, *Personnel Review*, Vol 7, No 2, pp36-39

Boxer, P J (1981a) Learning as a subversive activity, in Boydell, T and Pedler, M (eds) *Management Self-Development: Concepts and Practices*, Gower

Boxer, P J (1981b) Reflective analysis, in Shaw, M L G (ed) (1981) *Recent Advances in Personal Construct Technology*, Academic Press

Fransella, F and Bannister, D (1977) *A Manual for Repertory Grid Technique*, Academic Press

Hooper, R (1977) *National Development Programme in Computer-Assisted Learning: Final Report of the Director*, Council for Educational Technology

Musashi, M (1645) *A Book of Five Rings* Translated by Victor Harris in 1974, London: Allison & Busby Ltd

Shaw, M L G (1981) *Recent Advances in Personal Construct Technology*, Academic Press

CHAPTER 9

The Role of Reflection in a Co-operative Inquiry

John Heron, *British Postgraduate Medical Federation*

Co-operative Inquiry and the Experiential Learning Cycle

Co-operative inquiry (Reason and Rowan, 1981a) is primarily a way of doing research with people rather than on people. It breaks down the distinction between researcher and subject: the researchers are also co-subjects and the subjects are also co-researchers — everyone involved moves between both roles (Heron, 1981a). There are many arguments for doing research about people this way (Heron, 1981b): the primary one in my view is that it is the only way of researching people as fully self-determining, as beings whose thinking and choosing shapes their behaviour. If the subjects of research are not being self-determining in the research situation, that is, they are being directed by the researchers, then they are not being fully themselves. It is only when the subjects of research start to participate in the thinking that generates, manages and draws conclusions from the research — that is, when they become co-researchers — that they manifest within the research situation as fully self-determining people.

Seen in another light, co-operative inquiry is a way of systematically elaborating and refining an experiential learning cycle. The inquirers start as co-researchers with a phase of reflection, clarifying the initial idea of the inquiry and a method of conducting the inquiry. They then implement the method, as co-subjects, and enter a phase of action and experience. They complete the cycle by returning to a phase of reflection, to make sense of the action and experience and modify the initial idea accordingly. So it is a co-operative way of learning from individual and shared experience.

Thus in the first co-operative inquiry into co-counselling (Heron and Reason, 1981), the research group of co-counsellors decided to map out more thoroughly the different states of being clients go through during a co-counselling session. We met for three weekends at three-week intervals. During the first two weekends, we had a series of short co-counselling sessions. Each person immediately after a turn as client mapped out the series of states passed through during the session, with feedback from the counsellor. All these individual maps were shared and discussed and refined before the next co-counselling session, the whole process being repeated several times. During the final weekend the most developed individual maps were discussed, refined and amended by the group, and these collectively agreed and approved maps became the 'findings' of the inquiry.

Thus there was individual reflection on experience by each client immediately after his or her session, followed by a phase of shared reflection when individual maps were compared and contrasted. What was learned out of this shared reflection led immediately into a decision about what sort of mapping to do in the next co-counselling session. The final reflection phase sought to distil the learning that had accumulated over the whole preceding series of cycles between experience and reflection.

In co-operative inquiry the experiential learning cycle is systematically elaborated and refined because of the strong spotlight put upon the reflection phase in the cycle. Since inquiry is afoot, it is important in the reflection phase, when the inquirers are making sense of their recent experience, that they do not distort or misrepresent it. There is a concern to ensure that the reflection gives a valid account of the experience, makes veridical rather than illusory assertions about it, and draws appropriate conclusions. Hence some of us (Reason and Rowan, 1981b; Heron, 1982) have evolved a set of validity procedures that help reflection upon experience during co-operative inquiry move in the direction of truth rather than falsehood.

Aids to Valid Reflection on Experience

Research Cycling
If you go round the cycle of experience and reflection several times then you can progressively improve the validity of the reflection by testing and retesting it against the content of experience and action. You can repeatedly check your concepts for what they incorrectly include and omit. They may change through recycling, from the vague to the precise, from the obscure to the clarified, from the superficial to the deep and from the qualitative to the quantitative.

Divergence and Convergence
In the early stages of going round the research (experiential learning) cycle, it is wise for the inquirers to be divergent, that is to explore several different aspects of the experience being inquired into, to do so in diverse ways, and to reflect and report on these aspects in different ways. This is to ensure that reflection in later stages of the inquiry is not too narrow but has available to it a comprehensive array of data and varied and complementary perspectives, which can generate a holistic view. But if each inquirer on every cycle explores a different aspect, then no one aspect is ever taken round the research cycle more than once, so your final reflection may generate a widely holistic view although each of the conceptual bits are shaky. Hence the case, in later stages of going

round the cycle of experience and reflection, for being more convergent; that is, for all or several members taking certain aspects of the inquiry area through two or more cycles, in order to refine and improve reflection on those aspects. Convergence also means that in later stages of the inquiry your reflection phases are concerned strongly with how early divergent findings illuminate, complement, amend and correct each other. There are clearly innumerable ways in which divergence and convergence can be balanced and interrelated in the recycling process. The best balance is no doubt inquiry-specific.

Examples of Research Cycling, Divergence and Convergence
In the first co-counselling inquiry already referred to, each client in the early cycles was idiosyncratic and divergent, using any form of mapping to map whatever aspects of the session he or she chose. But since all the individual maps were shared after each co-counselling session, this meant that a good deal of convergent cross-fertilization led over into the planning of the next cycle. I might take up something you had learned from your last cycle into my intention for exploring and mapping my next session: thus there was an informal blending of divergence and convergence. Later in the inquiry we tried out two cycles, in each of which all of us converged on the same aspect of the client's session. At the end of the inquiry, in a very extended phase of convergent reflection in the group as a whole, we took the most coherent maps that different individuals had refined over previous cycles and amended and modified each one until all, including the originator, were satisfied. We reflected on how these several final maps supplemented each other, like photographs from different angles of the same building.

In a second co-operative inquiry into co-counselling (Heron and Reason, 1982), the inquiry group decided to explore how members handled restimulated distress emotion in everyday life when a co-counselling session was not available. We met once a week from 2pm to 7pm for shared reflection on the previous week's phase of experience, during which each member had reflection phases by keeping a regular diary of how he or she had handled restimulative incidents during the day. In the weekly group reflection phase, we shared our diary entries with each other, so again there was a good deal of informal convergent cross-fertilization from one person's past to another person's future phase of experience. The diary entries were (convergently) collated at each weekly meeting; and in the final convergent reflection phase these several collations were co-ordinated, then discussed and approved by the whole group.

In a co-operative inquiry into holistic medicine (Heron and Reason, 1984), 16 doctors met for two-day reflection phases at six-weekly intervals over a period of nine months. At the first reflection phase they developed a five-part conceptual model of holistic medicine; this was cashed out in daily professional practice divergently and idiosyncratically for the first two six-week cycles of action, with each practitioner exploring a different range of holistic strategies in his or her surgery. In the next three six-week cycles of action, there were two convergent sub-groups, one group taking strategies of doctor-patient power-sharing through three cycles, and another group taking spiritual intervention strategies in the surgery through three cycles. At the same time everyone kept some of their idiosyncratic strategies going from the first two cycles. In the last cycle everyone kept all this going, plus everyone using the same agreed form to identify the range of interventions used with any 100 consecutive patients. During the two-day meetings for the reflection phase it was a regular practice for the group as a whole to reflect on how this mass of divergent and convergent data influenced the five-part conceptual model generated at the outset. This act of convergent reflection was fully consummated in a final four-day reflection phase.

One thing I have learned from co-operative inquiries so far is that while there is a good deal of informal transfer of learning from one cycle to another — so that some sort of test and retest recycling of ideas goes on — it is quite difficult for a co-operative group to be fully intentional about the discipline of rigorous retesting and refining of strategic ideas through several cycles. The difficulty is in drawing the learning out of the previous phase of experience and action with sufficient acuity for it to be used to shape up clear intention for the next action phase. To put it crudely, the learning sometimes (but by no means always) seems to overflow from one action phase to the next, with people in the intervening reflection phase having a strong intuitive feel for what is going on and only a partial or limited intellectual grasp of the transfer process.

What aids both divergence and convergence are sharing and comment-or-feedback. In the reflection phase of the group, each shares recent past experience and how he or she has made sense of it: the resultant comparisons and contrasts between individuals' accounts will bring out both divergent and convergent aspects of these accounts. Similarly my comment on your account, and my feedback on your recent experience (if I were there at the time), will also throw into relief both different and similar perspectives. All this is essential for valid reflection, for holistic inquiry and learning. The truth is surely found where different perspectives converge to illuminate common ground. Unless you get enough difference or divergence, you will not get illuminating convergence.

Balance between Reflection and Experience
The validity of the reflection phase will in part be a function of how much reflection there is in relation to how much experience. Brief and cursory reflection upon deep and extended experience is not likely to yield up much truth-value; similarly with elaborate and prolonged reflection upon a fleeting trace of experience. A healthy time ratio will no doubt depend upon the sort of experience, and the quality and intensity of the reflection. A few moments of mystical experience may legitimate hours

of contemplative reflection; whereas many hours lying in an immersion tank may require only some minutes of reflection. An inquiry group will need to pay some attention to this from time to time and monitor the balance to see whether they have got it right. Since a good balance is so inquiry-specific, I do not think that any rules about it can be drawn up.

In the first co-counselling inquiry, each person had typically a 20-minute experience working as client followed immediately by a 15-minute reflection phase to make an individual map of that experience. This was then followed by perhaps an hour of a group reflection phase when all the individual maps were shared and compared. Thus the total reflection time was very much greater than the experience time. In the second co-counselling inquiry this sort of ratio was reversed. The experience phase was a week of restimulative incidents — small or large, few or many — and the reflection phase was a half-day a week for sharing and collating diary entries. In the holistic medicine inquiry, the experience phase was six weeks, with two-day reflection phases. Of course, in these last two inquiries, the experience phase contained sub-phases of individual reflection when each member was writing up a diary, keeping notes and records. In these three inquiries, the different time ratios seemed in each case to be about right. But especially in the last two mentioned, it may be that 'seemed right' was confounded with the virtual impossibility of changing the dates in everybody's diaries.

Authentic Collaboration
Since the inquiry is co-operative, validity in the reflection phase is also a function of how fully each person is contributing to the reflection, and how much each person is doing his or her own thinking and not merely echoing the views of one or more other people in the group. Only if there is maximal participation from everyone in each of these two senses, does the reflection phase derive the greatest benefit from the interaction of divergence and convergence. In the three inquiries mentioned above, individual reflection phases were built into the design: each person mapped a session, kept a diary and recorded work in the surgery. And in group reflection in each case there would be time, either in the whole group or in sub-groups, for each person to share individual reflections with the others. But after that, in more free-wheeling discussion in the whole group, contribution rates could start to get out of hand, with high contributors tending to take over the business of making sense of past experience and of planning forward. Thus there needs to be some conscious monitoring of contribution rates in these sorts of open discussion periods; otherwise collaboration can be restricted to a small group of dominant and articulate people.

Management of Unaware Projections
The notion here is that making sense of past experience during the reflection phase can be distorted by emotional distress that is stirred up by the inquiry process *per se* and by attendant phenomena of group

interaction, and so on. The whole business of communicating meaning, of being true to one's real and felt nature, of doing justice to what is actually going on, of honouring the reality of others, may not only generate anxiety and emotional agitation in present time; also it can evoke unresolved distress from early life when precisely these sorts of issues are so critical in the emerging identity of a young person. If such restimulated distress is not dealt with during the inquiry, it may be displaced unawares into the inquiry and cause lapses in motivation and commitment during the experience phase, lapses in diary-keeping and record-keeping during the individual reflection phases, confusion in getting at the real learning during group reflection phases and confusion in forward planning, cumulative interpersonal tensions that distort genuine co-operation and participation, and so on. I think I have seen all this occurring to a greater or lesser extent in the three inquiries mentioned.

Paradoxically, in the first co-counselling inquiry, we were so busy mapping client sessions on everything else that we did not include any sessions on distress evoked by the inquiry itself, until that distress caught up with us at the start of the last weekend meeting in an outbreak of dissatisfaction and confusion. We then took time out to co-counsel and to reflect on it.

In the second co-counselling inquiry we were alert to this issue from the start. However, since the focus of the inquiry was how to handle restimulated distress in ways other than having a co-counselling session, we were faced with a curious dilemma: if we discharged off the distress generated by the inquiry, then we undermined the objective of the research which was to study how we managed restimulation other than by emotional discharge; but if we did not discharge off that sort of distress, then maybe the validity of the inquiry would suffer if alternative coping strategies were ineffective. In the event, we decided to let each person deal with this dilemma as was felt to be appropriate — either taking time during our meetings for discharge or adopting non-discharge methods. Only one person during our meetings used the discharge approach, and this only once. I am still perplexed by the dilemma, but think on balance it would have been better to take time out during the meetings to co-counsel on inquiry-provoked distress, leaving the focus of the inquiry to be addressed in everyday life — which is really where the issue of handling restimulation without discharge arises.

In the holistic medicine inquiry, we dealt with the matter more fully. Every two-day meeting had built into it a two- to three-hour process group especially for members to deal with any tensions provoked by the inquiry: much of this was interpersonal, with episodes of personal work on regression and catharsis. We also had occasional co-counselling sessions. I do not think that by any means we dealt with all the unaware projections and displacements going on, but we kept the whole process reasonably sweet.

Falsification
One of the main problems about taking an idea down into experience

in order to test it and retest it, is that you have to be committed to the idea to want to do this. Additionally, since the idea defines the sort of experience you are to have, you have to believe in it sufficiently in order to gain the appropriate experience. Then again, once the idea has become clothed with your own experience, it becomes warm and endearing to you. For all these reasons you acquire a vested interest in not noticing the inadequacies of the idea in the face of experience. Hence the importance of falsification as a check on validity in the reflection phase.

What this means in each individual reflection phase is that you need to be vigilant in noticing how your ideas misrepresent your experience, by including what was absent in the experience or by excluding or distorting what was present. Thus you need to be in a state of 'alternative theory availability', not unduly wedded to any one set of ideas as a way of making sense of the experience. This is paradoxical, for if the experience is to be identifiable at all as a certain kind of experience, it is already clothed in some modest set of ideas.

In group reflection you can also use the sharing of others and, of course, the comment or feedback of others as an aid to falsification: what others say about their experience and their feedback on your experience or comment on your ideas, may show up ways in which your ideas misrepresent experience. But a good device in group reflection is a formal 'devil's advocate' procedure. In the holistic medicine group, we had a stick in the middle of the room during group reflection times. Anyone could pick up the stick and become formal devil's advocate, radically challenging the assumptions underlying the ideas being discussed, coming up with alternative and often reductionist ways of interpreting the data from experience. The idea of the stick was that by taking it up you were giving notice that you were engaging in a falsification test rather than expressing a personal point of view.

In a five-day co-operative inquiry into altered states of consciousness, we kept a record of each person's reports on what they had considered to be altered states arising from the various experiences we devised. Later in the inquiry we set up the following devil's advocate procedure. Each member in turn sat in a chair in front of the group and had read out all his or her individual reports of altered states. It was then open to anyone to come forward to give a critical, sceptical, reductionist account of any one or more of these reports, reducing the report of an altered state back to some misrepresentation of a quite ordinary state. The member whose reports were thus being reduced would listen carefully and then either (a) argue persuasively that the original account was more plausible than the reductionist account, or (b) hold on to his or her intuitive conviction of the validity of the account if it withstood the devil's advocacy, or (c) yield to the reductionist account if it honestly seemed more plausible.

Open Boundary Feedback
Some inquiries have closed boundaries: they deal with matters entirely

internal to their members, like the first co-counselling inquiry which was researching client states of members only. Others have open boundaries: in the experience and action phase people other than members are involved and affected, like the holistic medicine group whose members in the action phases were relating to their patients. Thus validity in the group reflection phase is clearly enhanced if there are some data on, and feedback from, those other people with whom inquirers interact at the open boundary. In the holistic medicine group members did contract to gather in patient feedback.

Chaos

One thing we discovered on the first co-counselling inquiry: it really is important for the group to be able to tolerate intermittent confusion, ambiguity, uncertainty, chaotic profusion of issues and possibilities and apparent difficulties. Otherwise there may be a tendency in group reflection phases for members to press for premature intellectual closure as a defence against the anxiety of the whole process. Clearly this is not in the interests of valid reflection. The group therefore needs to abide with the chaotic profusion for a while, and wait for a genuinely creative and illuminating order to emerge in its own time.

Sorts of Reflection Involved in Co-operative Inquiry

There is of course no absolute distinction between reflection and experience: the most abstract reflection is fed by the memory traces of past experience, and all perceptual experience has a conceptual dimension of interpretation and identification. Thus before dealing with the reflection phase, let me mention some relevant cognitive attitudes during the experience phase.

Open Awareness This is the bedrock of experiential knowing: bracketing off preconceptions and being fully open to the self in a situation and to the abundance of the experience — in its obvious and subtle aspects, at its surface and in its depths. There is probably an element of extra-linguistic awareness in this: to the extent that it is possible to enter that aspect of perception that is prior to the acquisition of, and underpins the revisionary use of, language. It is openness to process and presence as such, as pure morphology.

Phenomenological Discrimination This is a subtle cognitive activity that grows out of, and goes with, open awareness: identifying what is going on while it is going on, discriminating the contours, aspects and dimensions of the experience from within it. Where there is obscurity or ambiguity in the phenomena it may mean trying out different ideas for their ability to clarify or resolve perception. There can be on the spot falsification: seeing whether alternative ideas to those used in the experience do more justice to it. At a basic level this may mean moving to and fro between extra-linguistic and linguistic perception: moving between the experience as one of pure form and process and the experience as perceived within the categories that come with the use of language. This phenomenological discrimination may be exercised when a person is more passive and quiet in the experience phase, or – and this is rather more challenging – when a person is actively engaged with some performance or interaction with others.

This discrimination during experience requires a subtle balance of attention. If your attention is too caught up in the experience, too absorbed or hypnotized by it, then effective discrimination ceases. And if your attention gets too disengaged from the experience, then the experience becomes withered and reduced, and discrimination degenerates into dissociated, unsupported abstraction.

Active Choosing During the experience phase you will also have to make intelligent choices about how to carry your action forward. This means thinking creatively and flexibly about your next moves while acting in the middle of some developing situation. As with discrimination, a balance of attention is required: becoming too absorbed in current action may result in relatively blind 'choices'; while too much detachment may lead to vacillation or missed opportunity.

Sorts of Thinking Involved in the Reflection Phase

Now I come to some of the sorts of thinking involved in the reflection phase, many of which are interlocking and overlapping.

Loose Construing and Divergent Thinking These may tend to go together during reflection phases in earlier stages of the inquiry; nevertheless they are not the same. Loose construing means making sense of past experience with a light and loosely fitting set of concepts that let the experience breathe, that tolerate obscurities and ambiguities, that avoid premature intellectual closure. In early reflection phases it is better to be vaguely right than precisely wrong. Divergent thinking means considering diverse aspects and perspectives of the past experience, and in different ways. This too is particularly important in early stages of the inquiry, as I have discussed in some detail above. Both loose construing and divergent thinking may be aided by the three following processes.

Presentational Construing What I mean here is making sense of past experience in nonverbal ways, by drawing and graphics, by painting, by nonverbal demonstration, by movements, by mime, by sound and music. This can be done as a sort of learning in its own right, and also to loosen up creative, divergent verbal thinking. In the first co-counselling inquiry, members used a lot of graphics in making sense of their individual client sessions, and with good effect.

Free or Directed Association Making loose and divergent sense of past experience may be facilitated by associating freely or directedly to it. I do not think we ever used this formally and explicitly as an exercise in group reflection phases in any of the inquiries mentioned, but I think it would have been a good idea to have done so.

Use of Metaphor, Analogy, Allegory, Story-telling These are all ways of harnessing the power of imagination to yield subtle and comprehensive views of past experience. It can be argued that they unfold a dimension of truth *sui generis*, and also alert the discursive intellect to a more holistic analysis. I think that none of our inquiries adequately exploited their potential.

Qualitative Description and Theorizing These are two basic levels of reflection in the reflection phase. The first involves getting out a comprehensive set of basic phenomenal categories to describe the experience, covering pertinent aspects — clear and obscure, central and peripheral, obvious and subtle. The second involves some higher-order explanatory account of what has been going on as depicted by the phenomenal categories. They roughly coincide, respectively, with earlier and later stages in the inquiry; and with loose construing/divergent thinking and tight construing/convergent thinking.

Tight Construing and Convergent Thinking These may tend to go together during reflection phases in later stages of the inquiry, but are not the same. Tight construing means working for greater coherence and density in the conceptual framework that makes sense of the experience phases. Convergent thinking means reflecting on divergent aspects and perspectives, refining each and bringing out the common ground they illuminate.

Modes of Theorizing

Higher-order explanatory reflection may itself involve one or more different sorts of thinking, as follows (Reason and Rowan, 1981c):

Causal Thinking Yields explanations in terms of linear cause and effect sequences.

Systems Thinking Yields explanations in terms of patterns of interaction, of simultaneous dynamic mutual influence, which cannot be reduced to explanations in terms of linear cause and effect.

Dipolar Thinking Yields explanations that take account of the interdependence of polar opposites, that avoid unipolar reductionism.

Contextual Thinking Yields explanations that acknowledge that all interpretations of experience emerge out of a cultural and historical context.

Practical Thinking Yields practical knowledge about action of such forms as 'When we wanted to achieve B, then we did C', 'When we did X, then these intended or unintended consequences followed'.

The Experiential Ground of Reflection

The reflection phase can only work with the fruits of the experience phase, and everything depends on whether the inquirers are 'awake' or 'asleep' during the experience. They are awake if they are practising what I have described above as open awareness, phenomenological discrimination, and active choosing while they are up at the experiential frontiers. They are asleep if their attention becomes too identified with what is happening and they slip back into conventional, routine, habitual, *ad hoc* ways of being. If they stay awake they bring a large amount of fruit for reflective harvesting, whereas if they fall asleep there is a meagre yield.

Experience and Reflection as Mutually Enhancing

One of the important benefits that members of co-operative inquiries report upon is that the regular phases of group reflection enhance people's ability to stay awake during the experiential phases which, in turn, makes the group reflection more productive. The shared consciousness-raising that occurs during group reflection gives a great boost to sustaining the appropriate balance of attention during the phases of experience, and thus yields further benefit.

In the first co-counselling inquiry, several members reported that their co-counselling sessions, done as part of the inquiry, were more effective and penetrating as sessions: balance of attention for emotional discharge was better, picking up and moving on one's own cues were sharper. It seemed that the extra margin of awareness needed for practising phenomenological discrimination during the session improved the session. In the second co-counselling inquiry, members were more alert to the occurrence of restimulation in everyday life and more able to take charge of it in diverse ways other than emotional discharge in a co-counselling session. The moral seems to be that if we set out collectively to learn about certain sorts of experiences by moving several times between the poles of the experience and collective reflection upon it, then apart from what we learn, we also have higher quality experiences of that sort. This seems to be good news.

References

Heron, J (1981a) Experiential research methodology, in *Human Inquiry* (below)

Heron, J (1981b) Philosophical basis for a new paradigm, in *Human Inquiry* (below)

Heron, J (1982) *Empirical Validity in Experiential Research*, University of Surrey: Human Potential Research Project

Heron, J and Reason, P (1981) *Co-counselling: An Experiential Inquiry*, University of Surrey: Human Potential Research Project

Heron, J and Reason, P (1982) *Co-counselling: An Experiential Inquiry II*, University of Surrey: Human Potential Research Project

Heron, J and Reason, P (1984) New paradigm research and holistic medicine, *British Journal of Holistic Medicine*, 1, pp86-91

Reason, P and Rowan, J (eds) (1981a) *Human Inquiry: A Sourcebook of New Paradigm Research*, Chichester: Wiley

Reason, P and Rowan, J (1981b) Issues of validity in new paradigm research, in *Human Inquiry* (above)

Reason, P and Rowan, J (1981c) On making sense, in *Human Inquiry* (above)

CHAPTER 10
Action Research and the Politics of Reflection

Stephen Kemmis, *Deakin University*

It is the greatest irony of human progress that as humanity has increased its control of nature it has become immeasurably more vulnerable to the power and products of human thought itself. Despite our technological mastery of disease, hunger and hostile environments, our technologies threaten species, habitats, cultures and, through nuclear weapons, the entire world. Our social gains have been equivocal: enlightenment and egalitarianism have failed, thus far, to achieve a rational, just and fulfilling world order. The most insidious danger, it has been argued, is in the conventional modes of contemporary thought itself, especially those modes of thought characteristic of advanced Western society. The German social scientist Horkheimer believed that mass culture threatened the capacity for critical thought:

> In his book *The Eclipse of Reason* (1947), Max Horkheimer, founder of the Frankfurt Institute for Social Research, provided one of the most succinct formulations of the problem engendered by mass culture. According to Horkheimer, the significance of the challenge posed by the massified culture industry to civilisation as such consisted in its assault on the capacity to engage in critical thought as a meaningful form of social discourse. Horkheimer cared deeply about the content of critical thought, but with the rise of fascism he became more concerned with the spectre of the end of reason itself. In his view, the capacity of humans to distance themselves from the object in order to gain a critical perspective upon their social world can no longer be taken for granted. The restricted language and thought codes produced by the reduction of all thought to its technical dimensions reach far into the culture, encompassing schools as well as communications, the public as well as the private spheres of discourse. It is no longer a question of whether ordinary discourse is able to deal with specific ideological and social content. As Jurgen Habermas expressed it, the new situation raises the issue of the competence of people to effectively communicate ideational content. The issue is the capacity for theoretical or conceptual thought itself. When people lack such competence, social action that transcends the struggle for justice within the empirically given rules of social organisation and discourse is impossible. (Aronowitz, 1977, p768)

The 60-year research programme of the Frankfurt Institute for Social Research has generated a wide-ranging and disturbing critique of twentieth-century ideology. Much of this critique concerns the scientism of modern thought: the belief that science and technology can solve all our social, cultural and material problems. Like theology in earlier epochs, this belief in science frames the great enterprises of our time (in industry, agriculture, information technology, economics and social and educational research and development). These great enterprises create a context for individual thought and action, giving it a specific character and form.

Berger, Berger and Kellner (1973), writing about modernization and consciousness, provide convincing evidence that the thoughtways of modern industrial society, predicated on bureaucratic forms of social organization, factory production processes, and the privatized gratifications of consumption, lead to a profound form of alienation they call 'homelessness': an abstract and universalized form of thinking which undermines the concrete, contextually relevant and convivial thinking which relates members of communities to one another and to the cultural, economic and geographical locations which give their lives meaning and significance.

In parallel with Horkheimer's view that mass culture undermines our critical capacities, the literary theorist Lucien Goldmann points to an additional loss, the loss of concern with the possible:

> . . . of the two dimensions of existence, the actual and the possible, which characterise man, the possible, in which the essence of literary creation exists, is increasingly tending to disappear from men's consciousness, producing in the end what [Marcuse] calls 'the one dimensional man'. (Goldmann, 1968, p48)

Against this background, a book about reflection is a subversive text. It is, at least, an affirmation of the enlightenment spirit that human thought can strain against the shackles of mass culture, perhaps even break free. A book about reflection may contribute to the historical struggle to explode and transcend the contradictions of 'mainstream' society and culture.

My central thesis is that reflection is a political act, which either hastens or defers the realization of a more rational, just and fulfilling society.
I have seven points to make about reflection and the study and development of reflection:

1. Reflection is not a purely 'internal', psychological process: it is action-oriented and historically embedded.
2. Reflection is not a purely individual process: like language, it is a social process.
3. Reflection serves human interests; it is a political process.
4. Reflection is shaped by ideology; in turn, it shapes ideology.
5. Reflection is a practice which expresses our power to reconstitute social life by the way we participate in communication, decision-making and social action.
6. Research methods which fail to take into account these aspects of reflection are, at best, limited and, at worst, mistaken; to improve reflection, the study of reflection must explore the double dialectic of thought and action, the individual and society.
7. A research programme for the improvement of reflection must be conducted through self-reflection: it must engage specific individuals and groups in ideology-critique and participatory, collaborative and emancipatory action research.

I will conclude by presenting an example of emancipatory action research to illustrate the power of self-reflection and the promise of the action research approach for the development of reflection.

The Nature of Reflection

We are inclined to think of reflection as something quiet and personal. My argument here is that reflection is action-oriented, social and political. Its 'product' is praxis (informed, committed action), the most eloquent and socially significant form of human action.

Reflection is not a Purely 'Internal', Psychological Process: it is
Action-oriented and Historically Embedded
Because reflection goes on inside the head, as it were, we are inclined to think of it as an 'internal', purely psychological process. To do so is to ignore the very things that give reflection its character and significance: to split thought from action.

When we stop to think — to reflect — we do so in order to take stock of something that has happened, in order to prepare ourselves for action, or (usually) to do both. Reflection is a dialectical process: it looks inward at our thoughts and thought processes, and outward at the situation in which we find ourselves; when we consider the interaction of the internal and the external, our reflection orients us for further thought and action. Reflection is thus 'meta-thinking' (thinking about thinking) in which we consider the relationship between our thoughts and action in a particular context.

We do not pause to reflect in a vacuum. We pause to reflect because some issue arises which demands that we stop and take stock or consider before we act. We do so because the situation we are in requires consideration: how we act in it is a matter of some significance. We become aware of ourselves, in some small or large way, as agents of history; we become aware that how we act will influence the course of events, at least for ourselves and usually for others too.

Since Aristotle, it has been possible to distinguish three broad forms of reason on the basis of the way they relate thought and action: technical, practical and theoretical reason. Technical or instrumental reason concerns choosing between available means to achieve a known end. Its ideal type is the 'making' action of the craftsperson aiming to produce, for example, a pot of a known type for a known purpose. Aims-achievement criteria are available for determining when the job has been done and how well it has been done (the pot is finished, and it is suitable for its purpose). Practical reason, by contrast, takes place in a context where both means and ends must be considered, and where choices need to be made about the criteria by which to judge the action to be taken (and where there may be competing criteria by which to judge it). Its ideal type is the 'doing' action in which the actor must decide how to act rightly and appropriately in a given situation. The situation itself is risky (right and wrong actions are both possible), but it must be lived through. The person has no choice but to act as correctly as possible: history will judge how well. Theoretical or speculative reason (*theoria*) is simply the pursuit of truth through contemplation. In Aristotle's time, theoretical reason was philosophizing; in our time, it lives on in the aspiration of some forms of science ('pure' science) to be the pursuit of truth for its own sake (for example, in the justification sometimes given for pure mathematics), and in the classical aspirations of modern critical social science to achieve emancipation from irrationality, injustice and social fragmentation.

Using this Aristotelian classification, we may distinguish three parallel forms of reflection: problem-solving, practical deliberation and speculative thought. *Problem-solving* is technical; it identifies a problem as a problem of a certain character, and it envisages a solution which 'removes' the problem. Much of our reflection today is of this technical kind: we identify problems in the material and social world, envisage their solutions (the problem solved, a blockage removed), and consider the means available to us for their solution. We may choose between available means on the basis of the efficacy and efficiency of alternative courses of action.

Practical deliberation is a different form of reflection, extending beyond questions of means to the appraisal of whole situations. In practical deliberation, we must consider what will be right and appropriate. We consider how best to act in the situations as a moral question. While questions of efficacy and efficiency are not ruled out, they are not our primary concern; our primary concern is to decide what course of action will prove afterwards to have been the wisest and most prudent, most contributing to the good. Questions of conscience require practical deliberation.

Speculative thought is different again. Here, our reflection is concerned with thought itself. While, to Aristotle, speculative thought was pure contemplation, in modern times what constitutes theoretical reason has become more sharply delimited. It has been shown (for example, by Habermas, 1972) that thinking about thinking often turns out to be a species of technical reason (for example, technical questions in logic, technical questions about methodology in scientific research) or practical deliberation (for example, interpretive thinking). In critique, however, we transcend the strictly technical or practical as we consider how the forms and contents of our thought shape and are shaped by the historical situations in which we find ourselves. Critical reflection self-consciously employs a dialectical form: it seeks to discover how the form and content of thought has been given by history, and how history itself will be shaped by our praxis (action informed by critical reflection). The self-conscious critique of ideology undertaken by the Frankfurt School, in which science is criticized as ideology and the critique is used to discover limitations to reason itself, provides a large-scale example of critical reflection at work. The title of Martin Jay's (1973) history of the Frankfurt School, *The Dialectical Imagination*, makes explicit the dialectical character of critical reflection.

In each case, we can see that reflection is action-orienting. In each case, it has its meaning and significance in relation to a context or situation (a historical field of action), though each case takes a different view about the degree to which context is to be treated as problematic. In no case (technical, practical or critical reflection), can reflection be understood without reference to action or context. The significance of this insight, that reflection is action-oriented and historically embedded, is that reflection cannot be understood as purely 'internal' to the actor. To understand reflection, we must know, in specific instances, how actors are oriented to action by reflection, and how they orient themselves in relation to the historical field in which they must act. In reflecting, we orient ourselves as agents in history; we cannot understand reflection unless we understand its historical nature and function. As Benjamin Farrington observed:

> History is the most fundamental science, for there is no human knowledge which cannot lose its scientific character when men forget the conditions under which it originated, the questions which it answered, and the functions it was created to serve. A great part of the mystification and ignorance of educated men consists of knowledge which has broken loose from its historical moorings. (Farrington, 1949, p173)

Reflection is not a Purely Individual Process: Like Language, it is a Social Process

Once we have given up the view that reflection is something that goes on in the head, and recognized that it is a self-conscious process in which the thinker considers the relationship between his or her thought and action in real and determinate historical contexts, we can see clearly that it is a social process, not a purely individual process. Three observations are sufficient to convince us that reflection is socially located and oriented:

1. Sometimes we say that reflection is mind's conversation with itself. If not explicitly in language, at least we must admit that this conversation prefigures language.
2. The ideas and understandings which give form and content to our reflection are socially given: they come from a socially constructed world of meanings and significances (without which it is not possible to mean in any communicative sense).
3. The fruits of reflection — action — have their meaning and significance in a social world, in which others understand us through our actions (including our utterances) and, as Wittgenstein (1974) showed, in which we can invest meaning in our actions only by reference to the forms of life we share with others.

Consider my (technical, problem-solving) reflection this afternoon about the need to fix the light switch in my study: as I think about how to do it, I ask myself questions about whether I have another switch and how to replace the old one (using language); I employ my rudimentary knowledge of electricity and the lighting in my house (knowing something of lighting and light switches because I live in a social world in which lighting is significant); and I know that I will need a light in my study in order to work on this chapter (which has significance to me and to the editors of this book, at least). Or consider my (practical, deliberative) reflection on whether to refer, in this chapter, to the threat of nuclear arms: manifestly, I use language to think about it, I consider and debate the issue against the background of a debate about nuclear disarmament, and I choose to go ahead knowing that it will raise the issue once more for others. Or consider my (critical) reflection about reflection itself in this chapter: again, I depend upon language and upon the significance of the issue to readers, but I also aim to place the idea of reflection in a context of history and social theory (Aristotle, Horkheimer, and the rest) to remind readers that their views of reflection may have been shaped by a psychologized, technologized view of the world, and to suggest that we need to take hold of our ideas about reflection and to use them as part of a political struggle for a more rational, just and fulfilling society.

This insight, that reflection is not individual but intrinsically social, denies the view that the study of reflection is the preserve of psychologists and asserts that the study of reflection requires a comprehensive social theory including a view of social life and social action. It denies the possibility that reflection can be understood individualistically and asserts that a theory capable of understanding reflection must relate individual thinking to society and culture. It asserts that reflection is dialectical in a second sense: that the thinking of the individual is shaped by a social and cultural context, and that the social and cultural context is itself shaped by the thought and action of individuals. The study of reflection requires a critical science of society capable of comprehending this dialectical relationship between the individual and society.

Reflection Serves Human Interests: it is Political

In his book, *Knowledge and Human Interests* (1972), Jurgen Habermas showed that the search for knowledge was guided by interests (in the sense of 'self-interest') of different kinds. He distinguished three broad types of these 'knowledge-constitutive interests' (interests which guide and shape the constitution of knowledge), one associated with each of the Aristotelian forms of reason: technical, practical and emancipatory. The technical interest is directed towards control of nature. It generates instrumental knowledge (knowledge which codifies our means of control), often in the form of causal explanations. This knowledge may be accumulated and pursued through empirical-analytical sciences (on the model of the physical sciences). It assumes and envisages a medium of social organization in which this knowledge can be used: in this case, work. The practical interest is directed towards mutual understanding and wise action within a coherent framework of values. The knowledge it generates is in the form of interpretations of social life; it is pursued through the hermeneutic or interpretative sciences (on the model of history). The medium of social organization in which this interpretative knowledge has its significance is language (in which understandings between people are communicated and co-ordinated). The emancipatory interest is aimed at emancipating people from the dictates of taken-for-granted assumptions, habits, tradition, custom, domination and coercion, and self-deception. Here, Habermas aims to synthesize the classical concern for praxis (wise and prudent action) with the logical and theoretical rigour of modern science. He recognizes that the content and form of our thinking are socially constructed, but that we are also able to use our critical abilities to reconstruct what history and our development have constructed for us, and to construct new modes of thought and social action. The emancipatory interest is positively shaped by classical aspirations towards rationality, justice and fulfilment, but it must proceed negatively, as it were, by rigorous criticism of existing modes of thought and action (critique), searching always for new possibilities in which more rational, just and fulfilling forms of social life can be realized.

This critical thought yields knowledge directed towards human emancipation (critique); Habermas describes the science through which it is pursued as 'critical social science' (especially in the book *Theory and Practice*, Habermas, 1974). The medium of social organization for which such a science has relevance and through which it has its impact is the medium of power, in political organization. Figure 1 summarizes this classification of interests, knowledge, media of social organization and science.

Interest	Knowledge	Medium of Social Organization	Science
Technical	Instrumental (causal explanation)	Work	Empirical-analytic (physical sciences)
Practical	Practical (understanding)	Language	Hermeneutic or interpretative science (history)
Emancipatory	Critical (critique)	Power	Critical social science

Figure 1 *Summary of knowledge and interests*

The three forms of science to which Habermas refers (empirical-analytic, interpretative and critical) are institutionalized organizations for the pursuit of different kinds of knowledge in society. The knowledge-constitutive interests which are their impulses, however, are as characteristic of reflection as they are of science. Technical reflection, as we have seen, aims at problem-solving within a social context of the control of nature; practical reflection aims at wise action in a social context of judgement about what is right; critical reflection aims at recovering and examining the historical and developmental circumstances which shaped our ideas, institutions and modes of action, as a basis for formulating more rational ideas, more just institutions and more fulfilling forms of action.

In each case, reflection is political, in the sense that it takes place against a context in which the self-interests of different people will be differentially served. Technical reflection takes the social context for granted; it aims at the solution of problems, having at the outset some criteria by which a solution can be judged to be a solution; it serves the ends of those for whom the problem to be solved is a problem. Practical reflection aims at the discursive examination of criteria as well as of action; it judges the rightness of action in a social context and it serves the ends of conscience in a context of communicating and co-ordinating ideas of the good. Critical reflection aims to discover how criteria have come to be accepted, to analyse their historical and social formation, and to organize social action towards emancipation; it serves the ends of society by identifying how our thought and action have been distorted by ideology and redirecting our thought and action to overcome these distortions.

In no case is reflection apolitical. Each case serves human and social interests differentially. In many situations, we respond with technical, problem-solving forms of reflection. For these situations, we regard it as sufficient to achieve an agreed end (or an end we are willing to treat as agreed). In other situations, we respond with practical reflection, concerning ourselves with what is right without necessarily concerning ourselves with the analysis of the social and historical conditions under which our values were formed. In still other situations, we respond critically, concerning ourselves both with the social and historical shaping of our ideas, institutions and modes of action and with the organization of action to emancipate ourselves from past irrationality, injustice and dissatisfaction. What distinguishes these forms of reflection is not whether they are political, but the degree to which we treat their political context and character as problematic.

In the most sensitive social situations, we are acutely aware that we must make a critical response. In these situations, we make a self-consciously critical analysis of the kind described by Freire as conscientization:

> . . . the process in which people, not as recipients, but as knowing subjects, achieve a deepening awareness both of the sociohistorical reality which shapes their lives and of their capacity to transform that reality. (Freire, 1970, p27)

In such cases, our aim is simultaneously emancipation and social empowerment: the conscious and deliberate organization of self-reflection as a part of a political struggle towards emancipation from the irrational, unjust and unfulfilling.

This insight, that reflection is a political process in which we locate ourselves more or less explicitly as agents in the historical struggle against irrationality, injustice and unfulfilment, denies that reflection is quiet contemplation primarily of significance to the individual and her or his own interests. It asserts that reflection and the fruits of reflection locate us in the historical struggle for human emancipation, whether implicitly or explicitly. When we understand this, we will acknowledge that self-reflection, undertaken in collaboration with others, is part of the political process by which we may transform irrational, unjust and unfulfilling social structures. It is part of the process of emancipation. 'In the power of self-reflection', writes Habermas (1972, p314), 'knowledge and interest are one.'

Reflection is Shaped by Ideology; in Turn, it Shapes Ideology
Regarded as an object, ideology is the cultural and cognitive 'residue' of values, attitudes and beliefs which sustain a society economically, socially and politically by reproducing our ideas of how we fit into the life of society and, in particular, by reproducing the social relations of production in society. More dialectically, ideology is created and sustained through definite patterns and practices of communication (language), decision-making (power) and production (work) which create expectations and sustain meanings for people as they relate to one another in the whole matrix of social life.

On the basis of what has already been said about reflection as an action-oriented, historically embedded, social and political process, it should be clear that reflection is ideological. This is so, first in the sense that the form and content of reflection are shaped by the life of society and the social relations of production. Our ideas and the way we reflect betray our expectations about how our thinking will have its effect on society. Who our action is directed towards, who we believe our co-actors will be (and who we will act against), the specific modes and register of the language we use, and the issues we think about all locate us ideologically as people of a certain kind, striving towards certain things, and relating in definite ways to others around us.

Our reflection is also ideological in the sense that it sustains and reproduces or challenges and transforms these sets of relationships, modelling and creating either the same or different sets of relationships between people, and between people and the processes of production, decision-making and communication.

As we have seen in relation to the interests knowledge serves, reflection can orient us in very different ways to action. As 'meta-thinking' (thinking about the relationship between thought and action in a particular context), reflection expresses quite definite ideological commitments, taking certain aspects of social life for granted or treating them as problematic, and revealing an orientation to the social world and social order. When I reflect on the light in my study, I 'choose' not to consider the energy shortage or the significance of my work at my desk in relation to the division of labour between myself and the producers of the energy which lights my lamp. When I reflect on whether to mention nuclear war in this chapter, I choose to use this chapter as an opportunity to raise the question of social relations in our world society. When I reflect on reflection in this chapter, I aim to locate reflection as a moment in the historical process of emancipation and the transformation of irrational, unjust and unfulfilling social orders.

In reflection we choose, implicitly or explicitly, what to take for granted and what to treat as problematic in the relationships between our thought and action and the social order we inhabit. In reflection, we have a choice about whether to think and act in conformity with the patterns of communication, decision-making and action in our society, or whether we will intervene at this historical moment on behalf of more rational communication, more just decision-making and more fulfilling human and social action.

The insight that reflection is ideological in the sense that it is ideologically shaped and contributes to the shaping of ideology (by sustaining or challenging taken-for-granted modes of social relationship) asserts our agency as the makers of human history. It denies that we are merely determined as 'products' of our history and development; it also denies that we are entirely free to produce the world and the history we desire, regardless of the historical circumstances in which we find ourselves.

Reflection is a Practice which Expresses Our Power to Reconstitute
Social Life by the Way We Participate in Communication,
Decision-making and Social Action

Althusser writes:

> By practice in general I shall mean any process of *transformation* of a deter-
> minate given raw material into a determinate *product*, a transformation
> effected by determinate human labour, using determinate means of pro-
> duction. (Althusser, quoted by Bennett, 1979, p111)

Reflection is a process of transformation of the determinate 'raw material' of our experiences (given by history and culture, and mediated through the situations in which we live) into determinate products (understandings, commitments, actions), a transformation effected by our determinate labour (our thinking about the relationship between thought and action, and the relationship between the individual and society), using determinate means of production (communication, decision-making and action). Althusser argues that ideology is a practice: it exists in the social and individual processes by which we produce and reproduce or transform our culture, economy and political structures through the practice of our social relationships. Ideology may be transformed only by the transformation of our practices of communication, decision-making and action. To transform these practices is to transform ourselves as actors and to transform the social institutions of our society. Ideology 'gives' us our identities ('appellates' the individual, in Althusser's term) and gives meaning to the actions by which we create and recreate the social institutions we inhabit; we transform ideology by changing our identities as social agents and our practices as inhabitants of institutions. Reflection is a moment in this process of transformation.

When we pause to reflect, we raise the possibility of transforming the social world through our thought and action. We may choose whether to intervene to establish more rational forms of communication, more just processes and procedures for decision-making, and forms of work and social action which are more fulfilling and more likely to foster social solidarity.

As a practice, reflection may be improved. Just as reflection can help us to make problem-solving more efficient and efficacious, and to make practical deliberation wiser and more prudent, so critical reflection may be improved by our developing deeper analyses of the historical and social situations which frame our reflection and by studying the consequences of our reflective action for ourselves and the society in which we live.

The insight that reflection is a practice denies that it is a mechanism (by analogy with mechanisms for information-processing) or a purely speculative exercise in the construction of interpretations or meanings. It is to assert that reflection is a power we choose to exercise in the analysis and transformation of the situations in which we find ourselves when we pause to reflect. It expresses our agency as the makers of history as well as our awareness that we have been made by it.

The Nature of Reflection: Summary
On the basis of the five propositions I have so far advanced, we may summarize the nature of reflection as follows:

1. Reflection is not biologically or psychologically determined, nor is it 'pure thought'; it expresses an orientation to action and concerns the relationship between thought and action in the real historical situations in which we find ourselves.
2. Reflection is not the individualistic working of the mind as either mechanism or speculation; it presumes and prefigures social relationships.
3. Reflection is not value-free or value-neutral; it expresses and serves particular human, social, cultural and political interests.
4. Reflection is not indifferent or passive about the social order, nor does it merely extend agreed social values; it actively reproduces or transforms the ideological practices which are at the basis of the social order.
5. Reflection is not a mechanical process, nor is it a purely creative exercise in the construction of new ideas; it is a practice which expresses our power to reconstitute social life by the way we participate in communication, decision-making and social action.

The Study of Reflection

It might appear to some that no particular scientific study of reflection could hope to include all these aspects of reflection. On the contrary, my contention is that a study which fails to include any of them will not be a study of reflection at all and, in this sense, will not be scientific.

To Improve Reflection, the Study of Reflection must Explore the Double Dialectic of Thought and Action, the Individual and Society
The scientific study of reflection must include (i) consideration of the role of reflection in orienting action in specific, real, historical contexts; (ii) consideration of the social relationships presumed and prefigured in the thinking of the actor and the action he or she takes on the basis of reflection; (iii) consideration of the values and interests which frame the thinking and action of the actor at this time and in this context; (iv) consideration of the ideological foundations of thought and action for the actor in a specific situation or, more particularly, the degree to which the actor's ideas and actions will contribute to reproduction or transformation of the social order as it is expressed in the situation; and (v) consideration of reflection as a practice in this situation, including the nature of the actor's participation in the process of communication, decision-making and action in the situation.

I take it that the aim of scientific studies of reflection is the improvement of reflection. Lest this be taken as too uncontroversial a statement, I should add that I take this to mean something quite different from the aims of control or understanding of reflection. Again following Habermas's distinction of the types of science, it is possible to see how empirical-analytic studies might be undertaken with the aim of increased control of reflection (for example, to improve the technical efficacy and efficiency of problem-solving). Equally, one can see how interpretative studies might be undertaken with the aim of reaching empathetic understandings of reflection in a situation (understanding the actor as a person confronted with a certain situation requiring reflection) or the aim of reaching a hermeneutic understanding (understanding the act of reflection in its historical context). In both cases, however, I must conclude (a) that something less than the whole of reflection as outlined here is being studied, and (b) that these studies do not necessarily contribute to the improvement of reflection.

EMPIRICAL-ANALYTIC STUDIES
These construe their objects (the things being studied) as phenomena external to the observer, as things to be observed. As I have described it, however, reflection cannot be studied from the 'outside'. Crucial aspects of reflection are only accessible from the 'inside' of the actor and the act: the attitudes, beliefs, ideas, motivations, values, interests and commitments of the actor, and the processes of judgement by which she or he makes a personal 'reading' of the meaning and significance of the situation and possible actions in it. Moreover, empirical-analytic studies are bound to reify reflection as a distinct process or entity susceptible of 'improvement' only in an instrumental sense; that is, to treat it as a 'thing' that can be made more efficacious and efficient, as a general means to

unspecified ends. In doing so, such studies distort the nature of reflection, giving primacy to the thinking process and treating the historical location and the ideological character of reflection as secondary. The empirical-analytic approach to the study of reflection thus betrays its own ideological formation and interest: it construes the improvement of reflection merely as the control of reflection, either in the sense of rationalistic control by the actor over the performance of procedures for problem-solving, and/or in the sense of social control over the way situations are to be addressed (as systems which either promote or impede the attainment of given ends). The empirical-analytic approach to the study of reflection is ideologically formed, but it is not self-reference: by studying reflection as an object, the empirical-analytic approach obscures its own ideological interest in technical control. The findings of empirical-analytic studies in the area of reflection must be treated with the greatest caution: the generalizations they produce are derived from the study of particular situations (chosen or contrived because they are amenable to study) which may or may not be relevant to the particular situations in which we find ourselves pausing to reflect. They spuriously treat the process of reflection (problem-solving) as unitary (when, according to the description here, it varies in character and content depending on the nature of the situation and the degree to which the reflecting person chooses to treat it as problematic), and they technologize the criteria for evaluating reflection, as if these criteria applied to reflection in general (rather than particular kinds of problem-solving) and did not depend on the judgement of reflective actors, on the one hand, and judgements about the meaning and significance of specific situations, on the other.

INTERPRETATIVE STUDIES
These are concerned with the meaning and significance of occurrences; they aim at empathetic understanding or historical interpretation. In relation to the study of reflection, they are indispensable but insufficient. They aim to 'get inside' the thinking of the reflecting person, showing us how that person perceived the situation as he or she did, and (in this sense) why the person acted in a particular way in the situation. They may also educate us about the historical character of the situation being confronted by the person and the historical consequences which followed from her or his action. Most frequently, interpretative studies do one or other of these things, but not both. In aiming to educate us about reflection and its consequences, however, interpretative studies work by example: they interpret reflection for us. While we may find these interpretations apposite as we consider our own reflection, they are not compelling for our own reflection because they are not based on our own analysis of our own reflection in the situations we actually face. Interpretative studies of reflection may provoke self-reflection, but they are not founded upon self-reflection; they may persuade, but they do not compel.

We must be wary of the findings of interpretative studies of reflection because they need not be authentic: grounded in the experience of our own thought and action. They do not engage us in the improvement of our own reflection by systematic self-reflection (on the relationship between our own thought and action, and the relationship between ourselves and our social world) as participants in the processes of communication, decision-making and social action which frame our social world for us, and through which we constitute it as social actors (as agents of history and ideology).

Put briefly, empirical-analytic studies of reflection are objectionable because they take a limited view of reflection and treat it technically. Interpretative studies are insufficient because, while being educative, they do not involve us as participants in the improvement of reflection as a practice, through self-reflection on our own participation in processes of communication, decision-making and social action. My seventh proposition concerns forms of study of reflection which overcome these objections.

A Research Programme for the Improvement of Reflection must be Conducted Through Self-reflection: it must Engage Specific Individuals and Groups in Ideology-critique and Participatory, Collaborative and Emancipatory Action Research

Research methods appropriate to the study of reflection must take into account the whole character of reflection outlined in these propositions. Put briefly, they must take into account the double dialectic of thought and action, and the individual and society. That is to say, they must analyse concretely, for particular situations, the mutually constitutive relationship between thought and action which forms the subject matter of reflection in a particular case, and the mutually constitutive relationship between the actor and the social world of which he or she is part. In order to achieve this, adequate studies of reflection must have access to the thought-categories, commitments and action-orientations of the actor (through which he or she interprets the situation and in terms of which he or she is oriented to action in it). While clinical or therapeutic (interpretative) studies may yield interpretations of these things, their validity is only guaranteed in the reflection of the actor himself or herself: to be 'objectively' valid, they must be verified 'subjectively', that is, they must be verified as authentic by the actor.

The first consequence of this view is that any study of reflection (and especially any study of reflection which aims at the improvement of reflection) must be participatory: it must involve the participation of the reflecting person himself or herself. In order to be valid, it must engage the self-reflecting person.

A second consequence is that such a study must be critical. As Habermas remarks:

> The self-reflection of a lone subject . . . requires a quite paradoxical achieve-
> ment: one part of the self must be split off from the other part in such a

manner that the subject can be in a position to render aid to itself . . . (Furthermore) in the act of self-reflection the subject can deceive itself. (Habermas, 1974, p29)

In order to penetrate the conditions of self-deception and guard against it, self-reflection must be both 'inwardly' critical, in the sense that it reviews actors' own self-formative processes (on the model of psychoanalysis), and 'outwardly' critical, in the sense that it reviews the history of self-formation and seeks to locate the ideological causes of self-misunderstanding and the collective misunderstanding of social groups (on the model of ideology-critique).

A third consequence of this view of self-reflection is that it should be collaborative. Collaboration with others in the process of self-reflection offers the possibility of a further check on self-deception (though collective self-deception remains possible). But collaboration in self-reflection also allows individuals to examine and to analyse their own uncertainties and dissatisfactions with others who may share them. Moreover, collaboration allows those engaged in self-reflection to examine and improve their own interactions in communication, decision-making and common action. Groups established with the purpose of striving towards mutual understanding (in communication), consensus (through rational and democratic processes of decision-making), and fulfilling common work may then recognize distortions in their own processes of communication, decision-making and action through a shared process of self-critical inquiry. Looked at from the inside, the collaborating group thus becomes a field in which distortions in the group's own self-understandings can be critically analysed; looked at from the outside, the collaborating group becomes an enclave from which distortions in social life in general can be identified (as they come to bear on the self-reflective group).

It follows from this that the study of reflection through self-reflection must also be practical: it must lead to decisions and be tested in action. To quote Habermas again:

> Critique understands that its claim to validity can be verified only in the successful process of enlightenment, and that means: in the practical discourse of those concerned (Habermas, 1974, p2)

> The organisation of enlightenment initiates processes of reflection . . . Thus the theory that creates consciousness can bring about conditions under which the systematic distortions of communication are dissolved and a practical discourse can be conducted; but it does not contain any information which prejudges the future action of those concerned. The psychoanalyst does not have the right, either, to make proposals for prospective action: the patient must draw his own conclusions as far as action is concerned. (Habermas, 1974, pp38-39)

Since reflection is action-oriented (the dialectic of thought and action), it must be studied and analysed in action. It is improved through studying and interpreting the consequences of reflection in action. In this context, we speak of 'the spiral of self-reflection' (Grundy and Kemmis, 1983; Carr and Kemmis, 1983).

Finally, it follows that the study of reflection through self-reflection must be directed by an emancipatory interest, the knowledge-constitutive interest of critical social science. Fay describes critical social science this way:

> [Critical social science] is clearly rooted in concrete social experience, for it is . . . explicitly conceived with the principal intention of overcoming felt dissatisfaction. Consequently, it names the people for whom it is directed; it analyses their suffering; it offers enlightenment to them about what their real needs and wants are; it demonstrates to them in what way their ideas about themselves are false and at the same time extracts from these false ideas implicit truths about them; it points to those inherently contradictory social conditions which both engendered specific needs and make it impossible for them to be satisfied; it reveals the mechanisms in terms of which this process of repression operates and, in the light of changing social conditions which it describes, it offers a mode of activity by which they can intervene in and change the social processes which are thwarting to them. A critical social theory arises out of the problems of everyday life and is constructed with an eye to solving them. (Fay, 1977, p109)

Thus far, I have sought to show that the study of reflection through self-reflection converges with the project of critical social science. While reflection appears to be on one side of each of the two dichotomies of thought-action and individual-society, we see that thought and action and the individual and society are not dichotomous but that they are dialectically constituted: thought constitutes and is constituted by action; the individual constitutes and is constituted by society. The study of reflection merges 'outward' into the study of ideology; the study of ideology merges 'inward' into the study of reflection.

To study reflection, therefore, we must adopt the methods of ideology-critique and participatory, collaborative and emancipatory action research. (For a fuller account of the relationship between ideology-critique and emancipatory action research in critical social science, see Carr, W and Kemmis, S *Becoming Critical: Knowing through Action Research* Geelong, Victoria: Deakin University Press, 1983, especially chapters 5 and 6.)

Critical Social Science and Emancipatory Action Research

Who conducts critical social science, and in whose interests is it carried out? Institutionalized social research commonly serves the self-interests of an academic research community or the sponsors of research projects. When this is so, social research becomes part of the establishment and the ideologically given framework of society. To escape ensnarement within the structured framework of self-interests that constitute the established social order, a critical social science must first of all conceive its audience as wider than the community of social scientists and the managers of society. If it does not, it may merely serve the interests of these groups and, through them, the established interests of the wider social order. If it does so, it puts its central critical task at risk. Second, it must conceive its participants (the 'scientists') in different terms: while conventional social research relies on specialist researchers to carry out the research task on behalf of society (as part of the division of labour which is itself ideologically structured), a critical social science must engage ordinary participants in social life in inquiries whose function is to disclose the ideological processes and structures which condition their own practices. In critical social science, the scientists are both the subjects (researchers) and the objects (participants in social life) of inquiry.

Critical social science involves the formation of groups committed to their own enlightenment. While some social research is evaluated solely in terms of the theoretical adequacy of its formulations, and other social research is evaluated solely by its practical or technical achievements, critical social science requires that both of these criteria for evaluation be employed and that an additional criterion be added: the success of critical social science requires that the community of social participants-researchers achieve enlightenment in their own understandings and for themselves about the nature of the relationship between their own knowledge and action and about the nature of the relationship between their own social processes and those of the social order in general (ideology).

Habermas put it this way:

> The mediation of theory and praxis can only be clarified if to begin with we distinguish three functions which are measured in terms of different criteria: the formation and extension of critical theorems, which can stand up to scientific discourse; the organization of processes of enlightenment, in which such theorems are applied and can be tested in a unique manner by the initiation of processes of reflection carried on within certain groups towards which these processes have been directed; and the selection of appropriate strategies, the solution of tactical questions, and the conduct of political struggle. On the first level, the aim is true statements, on the second, authentic insights, and on the third, prudent decisions. (Habermas, 1974, p32)

Put another way, critical social science requires the separate but simultaneous development of scientific discourse, the development of understanding and insights, and the development of practical action. To achieve the separate and simultaneous development of these three functions, critical social science presupposes a community of participants-researchers committed to the critical development of their own social life: their practices, their understandings of these practices, and the institutions and situations they inhabit and constitute through their action. Such an approach to social science is emancipatory in the sense that it is aimed at overcoming felt dissatisfactions, unjust processes of social control and decision-making, and irrational processes of communication.

Critical social science is thus both 'outward-looking' and 'inward-looking'; it involves individuals and groups in reflecting upon the ideological formation of their ideas, processes of decision-making and action, and upon their own participation in the processes of communication, decision-making and action by which their own modes of social life are structured. It involves participants as researchers into the double dialectic of thought and action, individual and society.

A form of critical social science which meets this description is emancipatory action research. (For a discussion of the distinction between emancipatory action research and technical and practical action research, see Grundy and Kemmis [1983] or Carr and Kemmis [1983, chapter 6].) In education, emancipatory action research is increasingly being employed in such settings as those of school-based curriculum development, professional development, school improvement programmes, and school and systems policy development. It is a form of participatory research carried out by educational practitioners and others (initially by teachers, and increasingly in collaboration with students, parents, and support personnel in education systems) into their own educational practices. Action research is a form of self-reflective inquiry undertaken by participants in educational situations in order to improve the rationality, justice and satisfactoriness of (a) their own social and educational practices, (b) their understanding of these practices, and (c) the institutions and situations in which these practices are carried out. It is most rationally empowering when undertaken by participants collaboratively, though it is often undertaken by individuals, and sometimes in co-operation with 'outsiders' whose aim is to help participants develop their facility with, and understanding of, the action research process as a process of critical social science.

Emancipatory action research involves participants in planning action (on the basis of reflection); in implementing these plans in their own action (praxis); in observing or monitoring the processes, conditions and consequences of their action; and in evaluating their actions in the light of the evidence they collect about them (returning to reflection) as a basis for replanning and further action. This is the spiral of self-reflection composed of cycles of planning, acting, observing, reflecting, replanning, further action, further observation and further reflection.

Emancipatory action research is concretely critical, in the sense that it involves participants in critical reflection on particular, real practices; the particular, real understandings they have of their practices; and the particular, real, historical situations in which they carry out these practices. It is participatory, in the sense that the actors themselves are involved in the critical self-reflection (which often extends to engage others in the reflective process), and it is collaborative, in the sense that practitioners and interested others engage in communication, decision-making and action about the practices under inquiry, on the one hand, and about the action research process itself, on the other.

In terms of the three separate and simultaneous functions of critical social science in the mediation of theory and praxis outlined by Habermas (1974, ibid), emancipatory action research engages participants in the development of scientific discourse, the development of understandings and insights (the organization of enlightenment), and the development of practical action.

At the level of scientific discourse, collaborating action researchers are engaged in 'the formation and extension of critical theorems' about their practices, understandings and situations, in the sense that they articulate their own theories, in their own language, about how their own thought and action are interrelated, and about how their own thought and action are constituted by and contribute to the reproduction and transformation of the social order (ideology). At the level of the organization of enlightenment, those involved in the action research process systematically and deliberately create the conditions under which they may articulate, explore and test their understandings in action, through self-reflection. At the level of the organization of practical action, participants work together to reach decisions about 'the selection of strategies, the resolution of tactical questions, and the conduct of political struggle'; that is, they plan action together, they carry out action together, and they reflect together on the processes and achievements of their common action as a basis for further collaborative planning.

Like critical social science in general, emancipatory action research has an emancipatory knowledge-constitutive interest: it is aimed at overcoming felt dissatisfactions, unjust processes of social control and decision-making, and irrational processes of communication. It begins by establishing a commitment to these aims within the practices and processes of the participant-researcher group itself, and analyses the means by which distortions in communication, decision-making and social action directed at fulfilment are generated within the group as a consequence of the self-formative processes of members' own development, and from outside the group as a matter of ideological distortion in the wider social order. Emancipatory action researchers can learn much from the research of critical theorists conducting ideology-critique of the kind undertaken by the 'Frankfurt School' (based on the Frankfurt Institute for Social Research). Ideology-critique in general helps us to understand how the content and forms of our thought and action are shaped by ideology. This is the 'inward' critical movement in critical social science which considers the ideological formation of our own ideas and practices. But emancipatory action researchers, in the spirit of social science, cannot merely accept these interpretations from critical theory uncritically, nor treat them as valid for their own situations without further analysis. Action research is a necessary correlative to ideology-critique, both in the sense that it is grounded and authenticated in the life experience of particular groups and in the sense that it provides for the concrete analysis of ideology in the particular practices of particular groups at particular times (in this way, it throws up new problems for ideology-critique in general). It complements the 'inward' movement of critical theory with an 'outward' movement from concrete practices to ideology in general, and from particular local situations to the social order in general.

An Example of Emancipatory Action Research:
Jo-Anne Reid's Study of Curriculum Negotiation

I have made a number of points about the nature of reflection, the appropriate methods for studying reflection (through self-reflection), and the character of critical social scientific inquiry as a means of improving self-reflection and the practices by which we constitute social life in the situations we inhabit and in the social order in general. Throughout, I have emphasized the role of self-reflection in the exploration of the double dialectic of thought and action, and the individual and society. I will conclude with a brief account of an example of emancipatory action research which exemplifies some of these points. I am aware, of course, that I run risks of over-interpretation: of asking a single example to illustrate and sustain all my points even though the study concerned was conducted for specific, limited purposes in a practical situation where a particular teacher and students were concerned primarily with their own educational action. I have chosen the example because it is readily available (it is reported in Boomer, G (ed) (1983) *Negotiating the Curriculum*, and in Kemmis, S *et al* (eds) (1983) *The Action Research Reader*) and because it is a modest and practical example of critical self-reflection at work, not specifically designed to exemplify the views of reflection and self-reflection I have outlined here.

The example is Jo-Anne Reid's study of negotiating the curriculum (Reid, 1983). It recounts an investigation into the problems and potential of curriculum negotiation in a year 9 English class in a Perth secondary school. The study involved Reid, an advisory teacher (normally working as a consultant to other teachers) in an investigation into the role of language in learning in the classroom.

A National Working Party of the Role of Language in Learning (see Boomer, 1983, for a description of the work of this group) had been established in 1977 by the Curriculum Development Centre in Canberra, and had provided an opportunity for a co-ordinated exploration of issues related to the role of language in learning by advisers and teachers around Australia. Of particular concern to the Working Party was the notion that students learn through using language; it followed, then, that teaching and learning strategies which recognized and extended children's own language could more surely engage children in particular learning tasks and more surely contribute to learning by recognizing what the children already knew (as this was expressed in and mediated through their own language). From this proposition, the slogan 'negotiating the curriculum' was fashioned. In a negotiated curriculum, teachers would invite students to reflect on what they already knew about a topic, to decide what else they would like to know about it, to consider ways they might find out what they wanted to know, to implement plans to find out more after negotiation with peers and teachers, and to evaluate the success of their inquiries by reflection on what they had learned in the light of their initial aims and plans. (These steps in the process of curriculum negotiation bear strong similarities to those of the spiral of self-reflection in action research.) The teacher would function in these inquiries as a stimulus for students, provoking reflection; as a resource, providing ideas and information when it seemed helpful; and a constraint, limiting the scope of inquiries by relating individual student plans to one another (to create opportunities for student collaboration) and to areas in which the teacher was willing and able to function as a resource.

As an English teacher, Jo-Anne Reid was aware of the work of the National Working Party, and she believed that its general principles about the relationship between students' language and their learning were right and appropriate. They were also practicable. She was interested to explore them further for herself in the classroom, however, and, in particular, to explore the idea of curriculum negotiation. She thus 'borrowed' a class of 34 year 9 students for 16 periods (over eight weeks in 1979). This would allow her to explore curriculum negotiation for herself, as one of a group of English teachers and consultants exploring the role of language in learning and curriculum negotiation in Perth at that time.

Curriculum negotiation involves giving students a voice in the choice and development of learning opportunities in the classroom; both the 'what' and the 'how' of curriculum. As a stranger to the class, Reid needed a topic area which could interest the students fairly rapidly; it was the International Year of the Child, so Reid chose the topic 'Kids in Schools'.

on the assumption that this was one situation that everybody in the class would
(a)   have direct experience of,
(b)   have formed personal opinions on,
(c)   be able to relate directly to themselves, and therefore,
(d)   find a non-threatening area to examine with a stranger. (Reid, p128, in Kemmis *et al*, 1983)

In the spirit of negotiating the curriculum, Reid was thus constituting the class as a reflective and self-reflective community of participant-researchers.

By choosing an inquiry topic which the students could relate to directly, Reid created conditions under which they could reflect on their own experience (and, as the work progressed, on their own processes of reflection and inquiry), and was able to create a convergence between her educational aim of fostering reflection among students and her own (self-educational) aim of self-reflection on strategies for curriculum negotiation.

Reid was thus creating conditions in which five separate levels of reflection were being organized:

1. Students' substantive reflection on the topic of 'kids in schools'.
2. Students' self-reflection on the processes by which they pursued their investigation of the topic (which also, by the way, allowed them to explore their insights about what they found out about 'kids in school' as they came to bear on their own processes of investigation in the exercise).
3. Reid's reflection on the practices involved in negotiating the curriculum in this specific case (Reid as teacher).
4. Reid's reflection on these practices as educational practices within the broader framework of strategies for English teaching with which she was concerned as an advisory teacher in English (Reid as advisory teacher).
5. Reid's self-reflection on her own processes of reflection and inquiry (Reid as teacher-researcher).

At each of these levels, participants were collaboratively involved in reflection and self-reflection (planning, acting, observing and reflecting together).

It is clear from the account this far that Reid was fulfilling the conditions of participation and collaboration characteristic of critical social science.

Following the model of curriculum negotiation, Reid asked the students to list what they knew about school, and then to list what they did not know but wanted to find out. She then asked them to decide how to find answers to the questions they had posed for themselves, through discussion and group decision.

Throughout the process, the students kept journals recording their activities and progress, as did Reid herself. These data provided a documentary record but also provoked and recorded self-reflection about the processes all were engaged in. The collection of this evidence promotes the attitude of self-reflection (distancing) as well as providing material for it. Keeping a journal helps participants to become 'reflexive spectators' (as Bev Beasley, 1981, puts it) who reflect on their actions and transform their ideas and their future action in the light of reflection. In these ways, the study was beginning to develop a critical perspective: it was creating the conditions under which the participants could consider their own interests (as students, teacher, etc) and perhaps, how they related to wider social interests.

Perhaps also, the topic 'kids in school' (for the students) and 'the negotiated curriculum' (for Reid and the other teachers and advisers she worked with) began to provoke an emancipatory interest in how schools and teaching are shaped and formed (that is, in ideological questions) and in how they might be made better (through changing conditions of communication, decision-making and educational action). It is difficult to say whether or how far this emancipatory intent developed on the basis of Reid's report, but clearly the topics invited self-reflection along these lines.

There is no doubt, however, that the study was practical: for students and teacher alike, it engaged them in considering their own practices (as students and as teacher), and in modifying their practices in the light of their reflection and self-reflection. For students, it provided an opportunity to think about their learning practices and the conditions of their learning. For Reid as a teacher, it provided an opportunity to reflect on the practices of negotiating the curriculum; for Reid as advisory teacher, it provided an opportunity to reflect on curriculum negotiation in relation to other teaching practices in English; for Reid as teacher-researcher, it provided an opportunity to reflect on action research as a way of improving teaching.

The study involved several cycles of planning, acting, observing and reflecting, with reflection providing a basis for planning what to do next. The study produced several sets of 'findings':

1. At the level of the students' investigation of 'kids in school', it

produced insights for students which they presented to students at a nearby primary school.

2. At the level of student self-reflection on the inquiry process, it produced conclusions about their own participation in the process, and evaluations of inquiry as an approach to learning.

3. At the level of reflection about negotiating the curriculum as a strategy (Reid as teacher), it produced insights about the problems and prospects of the approach.

These first three sets of 'findings' are quite explicit in the report. Two further levels are present, but implicit:

4. At the level of reflection on English teaching and the role of language in learning, the report contains reflections on the nature of students' writing and talk in the context of the negotiated curriculum; these comments presume an interested and critical community of fellow English teachers.

5. At the level of self-reflection on the action research process, the report provides information and commentary for others interested in teacher-research (for example, comments about data-gathering techniques and the difficulties encountered: problems of audio-taping, problems with the regularity of journal-writing, and problems of ensuring time for reflection).

I have avoided being explicit about the findings of Reid's study. They are findings relevant to a particular action research project undertaken in a particular context for particular purposes. Readers may, of course, find out more about them by reading the report. I have been inexplicit because the study demonstrates that emancipatory action research is concerned with reflection for the empowerment of particular people (in this case, students and teachers) in particular situations.

More widely practised, and with greater collaboration with co-participants, emancipatory action research offers real potential for the development of a critical social science of the kind described by Fay (1977). Practised in a thoroughgoing way by people committed to critical self-reflection and emancipation from the dictates of habit, custom, domination, self-deception and ideology, it can provide a method for reflection on the double dialectic of thought and action, and the individual and society.

Jo-Anne Reid's study lends support to the view that emancipatory action research can provide an appropriate method for the development of reflection through self-reflection. In relation to the propositions about reflection which have been the burden of my presentation, her study shows how action research can help individuals and groups to consider:

1. The role of reflection in orienting action in specific, real, historical contexts.

2. The social relationships presumed and prefigured in the thought and action of specific actors in specific situations.

3. The values and interests which frame actors' thoughts and actions in the specific situations in which they find themselves (the politics of situations).
4. The way actors' thoughts and actions contribute to the reproduction and transformation of the social order in general as it is mediated through the ordering of specific situations (ideology).
5. How, in practice, reflection bears on the actors' participation in communication, decision-making and social action, and thus expresses their personal power as agents of history working towards the creation of a more rational, just and fulfilling social order.

The systematic and self-conscious development of self-reflection through emancipatory action research may provide an antidote to the ensnarement of people in the privatized, scientific, alienating ideology of our time. If this is so, it may be truly subversive of our present irrational, unjust and unfulfilling social order, and assist in the transformation of this social world towards a world which is more rational, just, fulfilling and safe, not only for us but also for those who will inherit the history we are making today.

References

Aronowitz, S (1977) Mass culture and the eclipse of reason: the implications for pedagogy, *College English*, **8**, pp768-774

Beasley, B (1981) The reflexive spectator in classroom research. Paper presented at the Annual Meeting of the Australian Association for Research in Education, Adelaide, 11-15 November

Bennett, T (1979) *Formalism and Marxism*, London: Methuen

Berger, P, Berger, B and Kellner, M (1973) *The Homeless Mind: Modernisation and Consciousness*, New York: Random House

Boomer, G (ed) (1983) *Negotiating the Curriculum*, Sydney: Ashton Scholastic

Carr, W and Kemmis, S (1983) *Becoming Critical: Knowing through Action Research*, Geelong, Victoria: Deakin University Press

Fay, B (1977) *Social Theory and Political Practice*, London: George Allen & Unwin

Freire, P (1970) *Cultural Action for Freedom*, Cambridge, Mass: Center for Study of Development and Social Change

Goldmann, L (1968) Criticism and dogmatism in literature, in Cooper, D (ed) (1968) *The Dialectics of Liberation*, London: Pelican

Grundy, S and Kemmis, S (1983) Reader 'Action research in Australia: the state of the art (an overview)', in Kemmis, S *et al* (eds) (1983) *The Action Research Reader*, Geelong, Victoria: Deakin University Press

Habermas, J (1972) *Knowledge and Human Interests*, trans J Shapiro, London: Heinemann

Habermas, J (1974) *Theory and Practice*, trans J Viertel, London: Heinemann

Jay, M (1973) *The Dialectical Imagination: The History of the Institute for Social Research and the Frankfurt School, 1923-50*, Boston: Little, Brown & Co

Kemmis, S *et al* (1983) *The Action Research Reader*, Geelong, Victoria: Deakin University Press

Reid, J (1983) Negotiating the curriculum, in Kemmis, S *et al* (eds) (1983) *The Action Research Reader*, Geelong, Victoria: Deakin University Press. Also in Boomer, G (ed) (1983) *Negotiating the Curriculum*, Sydney: Ashton Scholastic

Wittgenstein, L (1974) *Philosophical Investigations*, trans G E M Anscombe, Oxford: Basil Blackwell

Index

Printed in the United Kingdom
by Lightning Source UK Ltd.
115190UKS00003B/19-30